The POETICS of LAND & IDENTITY among British Columbia INDIGENOUS PEOPLES

CHRISTINE J. ELSEY

FERNWOOD PUBLISHING • HALIFAX & WINNIPEG

Editing & text design: Brenda Conroy
Cover design: John van der Woude
Printed and bound in Canada by Hignell Book Printing

Published in Canada by Fernwood Publishing
32 Oceanvista Lane, Black Point, Nova Scotia, B0J 1B0
and 748 Broadway Avenue, Winnipeg, Manitoba, R3G 0X3
www.fernwoodpublishing.ca

Fernwood Publishing Company Limited gratefully acknowledges the financial support
of the Government of Canada through the Canada Book Fund and the Canada Council
for the Arts, the Nova Scotia Department of Communities, Culture and Heritage,
the Manitoba Department of Culture, Heritage and Tourism under the
Manitoba Publishers Marketing Assistance Program and the Province of Manitoba,
through the Book Publishing Tax Credit, for our publishing program.

Library and Archives Canada Cataloguing in Publication

Elsey, Christine J., 1953-
The poetics of land and identity among the Indigenous peoples
of British Columbia / Christine J. Elsey.

Includes bibliographical references and index.
ISBN 978-1-55266-550-3

1. Native peoples--Land tenure--British Columbia. 2. Native
peoples--British Columbia--Ethnic identity. 3. Native peoples--
British Columbia--Folklore. 4. Folklore--British Columbia.
5. British Columbia--Social life and customs. I. Title.

E78.B9E47 2013   971.1'00497   C2012-908247-3

Contents

Acknowledgments

Igratefully thank the people from the many First Nations of British Columbia who have shared their knowledge, wisdom and insights with researchers and academics since the turn of the last century. Their generosity has made this work possible.

I thank the people of Bella Bella, B.C., who introduced me to their culture when I was a youth living in that area and working for Central Native Fishermen's Co-op. Their kindness was unparalleled, as was their understanding of my young life. I thank the many people of the Lytton First Nation, in particular Chief Ruby Dunstan and the Dunstan family, for hosting me at their many gatherings and medicine circles from 1988 to 1995 and for sharing their insights and hospitality with me during that time. Their generosity, determination and grace inspired me to embark on this study.

I thank the Honourable Gwen Point for her many visits to my classroom to speak on Stó:lō spirituality and culture at the University of the Fraser Valley. Her insight and heart was another inspiration which encouraged the development of this work. I acknowledge the many First Nations leaders — too many to list — who have touched my life and influenced my thinking on Aboriginal rights and the meaning of land for the First Nations peoples in British Columbia. Special thanks and recognition must be extended to Chief Leonard George, of the Tsleil-Waututh Nation, whose many speeches, dances, songs, talks, lessons and neighbourly encounters (as a fellow resident along the Burrard Inlet over many decades) helped me reach an appreciation of First Nations spirituality and worldview. I acknowledge my late maternal uncle, Alon Williams, of Victoria, who shared with me the stories of his childhood experience of being cared for and taught by his maternal grandmother, Elizabeth Cumatatqua Joseph (originally of Xaxli'p First Nation, also known as Fountain, in Stl'atl'imx' territory, and later from Soda Creek). Alon shared with me his grandmother's teachings and stories from the Lillooet culture and talked to me in depth about my own Stl'atl'imx' heritage. For this I am very grateful, as it gave me the impetus to carry out this research.

I acknowledge Professor Ian Angus, supervisor for my 2001 doctoral dissertation, for his guidance and insights on European phenomenology and his interest in its relationship to Indigenous peoples. I offer thanks to my university colleague and friend, ethnographer Dr. Douglas Hudson, for our many discussions about the research he conducted for over three decades within many B.C. First Nations communities and for his continued interest in this project. My gratitude goes to Jean Wilson for both her encouragement and assistance in getting this work published. And I give special mention to Lee Philips, my assistant, who attended carefully to drafts in the editing process and graciously looked after the formatting of the manuscript. Lee gave generously of his time and was in every sense my right hand in the technical preparation of the manuscript, and for this I am very grateful.

I acknowledge the contribution and support of my family, both extended and near, and especially my children, Juliann and Emma Elsey-McCandless, for their patience during the research and writing process, which continued throughout their childhood. I acknowledge and thank their father, my former partner, John McCandless, for his dedication to the First Nations people of Lytton, his perseverance and energy in Stein Valley preservation, his dedication to First Nations' rights fulfillment and for sharing with me his valuable insights on First Nations politics over many years.

I thank Evelyn Roth, Chief Leonard Andrew and professors Gary Teeple and Marilyn Gates for their contributions to my intellectual life at an earlier stage. I acknowledge my late grandparents, Dr. Roy and Isabelle Elsey, for providing me with an interest in writing and language and the determination to think through a problem to its completion, as well as my friend and mentor, artist Ingrid Baxter, for her encouragement of my early intellectual inquiries.

My thanks for the help provided by Errol Sharpe and the editors and staff at Fernwood Press. Their support and comments in the editing process were invaluable.

Last but not least, I thank my parents, Pam and Jack Elsey, for their tireless support of my pursuits, both academic and cultural, their assistance with childcare, their endless encouragement in ways too many to write down here.

To each and every one of you, I am grateful.

Chapter 1

The People in the Land
and the Land in the People

This book addresses the clash of meaning and being between colonial institutions and First Nations. In order to indigenize mainstream government institutions (such as the Ministry of the Environment, parks, the treaty process, land claims cases before the courts, the Ministry of Forests and other government agencies and departments), it is important to recontextualize First Nations' landscapes (their traditional territories) as cultural heritage and as part of the people themselves. This book studies how cultural features embedded in oral tradition and folklore are expressive of the spiritual connection that many First Nations people have with their landscapes. I explore the meaning of land in terms of its emotional/spiritual value for the various First Nations of British Columbia, on the basis of what I refer to as "terrestrial poetics."

In 1989, the Xeni Gwet'in launched a series of legal actions which culminated in a ground-breaking and important title and rights case, known as the Williams case (Friends of the Namaiah Valley 2012). According to Ian Gill, in the mid-1980s, a story in the *Vancouver Sun* told of a "rare coalition of Indians, trappers, homesteaders, ranchers and hunters [standing firm against logging in their region] Of the six Tsilhgot'in communities that would go on to form the Tsilhgot'in in National Government, the Xeni Gwet'in First Nation would emerge over the next quarter decade as one of the most resolute advocates for indigenous rights and title" (Gill 2009: 126).

The appeal of the Xeni Gwet'in T'silqotin with respect to their claim of the Britany Triangle[1] (which took place in Vancouver on November 17, 2010) clearly showed the faint hope for indigenization of the court process. The Crown's notions of Aboriginal "title and rights" were freighted with Eurocentric values. In other words, the definition of "Aboriginal title" itself is on trial in British Columbia courts, and presently little agreement exists within the legal profession to clarify the matter. The Crown's definition of title did not correlate, even remotely, with the Xeni Gwet'in's meaning of land and territory. Whereas the Xeni Gwet'in felt an ancestral connection to the entire use-area that made up their traditional territory, the Crown wished to query their land claim on Eurocentric grounds of continued and unbroken occupancy and use. The court pushed for proof of exclusive ownership, or demonstrable proof of Xeni Gwet'in control of the region and their historical ability to keep others out — as would fit European definitions of state boundaries. To the Xeni Gwet'in, territorial control is a foreign concept and, although they used all of what the Crown was referring to as the "opinion area"[2] for hunting and food getting, it was not used continuously or even frequently. The Xeni Gwet'in argued for rare but ongoing use of the area and also claimed it was not their way to try to keep others out. They nevertheless related to it as ancestrally their own, demonstrable through ancestral territorial water flows, fishing streams, animal movements, oral tradition and family relations (Xeni-Gwet'in hearings, November 17, 2010).

The Xeni Gwet'in claimed an ancestral and emotional connection to their entire territory, as lived and felt, based on what they knew from their ancestors and on where they knew they could go. Their use of the territory was flexible. The Xeni Gwet'in were puzzled that Judge Vickers drew a straight ruler line through their traditional territory and confirmed the claim based on the 70 percent of their territory that sat on one side of it. The Xeni Gwet'in's objection to Judge Vickers' explanation of their territory showed the absurdity of Vickers' ruler line, which had no relevance to ancestral water flows, did not demonstrate their watershed, nor had any significance to their ancestral fishing streams. It was foreign in terms of anything the Xeni Gwet'in understood. Nevertheless, the Xeni Gwet'in had used what the Crown referred to as the "opinion area" for their food getting practices on certain years, and their elders and their oral tradition indicated that it was theirs. Therefore, the Xeni Gwet'in judgment, a watermark moment for Indigenous title and rights in Canada, was less so for the Xeni Gwet'in, who struggle with ongoing frustration due to false definitions, un-honoured claims and the pain of not being believed by the Crown. For example, a correct reading of Aboriginal title that overlooks ancestral stories, fishing places and water flows could see a family alienated from their treasured, hereditary fishing spot, which they had ritually cared for and worked for hundreds of years. Thus, we see that honouring the stories and oral tradition is paramount, as the land is wrapped in narrative and oral accounts that give testimony to the life and work of the people themselves.

After attending a Xeni Gwet'in hearing in winter 2010, I acquired a clearer picture of how difficult crosscultural translation is within Canadian institutions — the courts being a strong example. The Xeni Gwet'in peoples have used their land in their own unique Indigenous manner for countless generations. In spite of the optimism of the *Delgamuukw* (1997) and *Xeni Gwet'in* (2007) judgments that Aboriginal title exists and must be upheld through the obligation to consult with First Nations on the regions which they claim and that oral evidence must be respected, the nature of what constitutes a title or claim is still under litigation and appears to be at a stalemate. All this begs the question of the need to "indigenize" government processes, based on an understanding of hunting and gathering groups, and the need to provide culturally specific meanings of culture and territory for each First Nations society, based on their own collective story. In fact, on the day I spent in court, culturally specific models of land use occupancy and title were lamentably superseded by non-Indigenized, Eurocentric translations and meanings.

In the case of British Columbia's Indigenous peoples, oral depictions of the landscape reveal a thorough articulation of use-sites, sacred areas and territorial boundaries for each First Nation as shown in their many creation stories, such as the Transformer tales. These stories of origin are the timeless purveyors of cultural meaning and selfhood that serve to contextualize and traditionalize an entire people within the ancientness of their surroundings, to which, over centuries, they have become profoundly self-identified. Throughout this book, I give many crosscultural comparisons by reviewing extant stories and art relating to specific First Nations landscapes, demonstrating how, in each case, the stories represent a moment in the emergence of what constitutes the world for the people within that territory. Scholars of the philosophical school of European phenomenology, among others, argue that the dominant worldview of the North American mainstream, which flows from Western scientific thinking, presents a fragmented and rationalistic view of the universe, due to what can be called "scientistic," or analytic, thinking. Thus, phenomenology has been useful throughout this study as it problematizes Cartesian dualism, with its opposition of subject versus object, mind versus body and self versus other, which, since the time of the Enlightenment period in European history, has represented the ontological categories that characterize the Occidental self. Rationalism, as typical of the Enlightenment tradition in general, focuses on the natural world in terms of the insidedness and outsidedness of individual empirical bodies, thus placing the elements of nature into a series of analytic categories that are exterior and separate from humans. Such an intellectual legacy carries strong consequences for the Occidental perception of self, which is now predicated on the opposition of subject and object and the resultant ontological separation of individualistic humans from all other features of their worldly existence.

According to Nuu-chah-nulth scholar Richard Atleo, the Western pattern of thinking compartmentalizes experience:

> Yet from the outsider's perspective such as mine, I find it doubtful that holistic thinking could be considered an overriding theme in patterns of Western thought. There is instead a prevailing tendency to compartmentalize experience and thus assume that some parts

have no relationship to other parts. For example, in "Philosophers on Education: 6 Essays on the Foundation of Western Thought," Brumbaugh and Lawrence [1963: 36] state; "The world abounds in separations which have been overdone, which ignore the basic character of the experiential continuum." (Atleo 2004: xii)

Both phenomenology and Indigenous scholarship argue that, within the Occidental constructions of the physical world, such analytic and classificatory thinking patterns result in an ontological fragmentation which tends to minimize the importance of lived experience (or what could be described as the human factor) (Heidegger 1962; Merleau-Ponty 1962, 1968; Atleo 2004). Within the rationalist perspective, the human, spiritual, oral and experiential values of our environmental surroundings are awarded a low priority and are made insignificant within the enterprise of human knowledge and in the evaluation and understanding of the material and natural worlds (Evernden 1985). According to Indigenous scholar and researcher Kathleen Absolon, an Indigenous process of knowledge collection is generally experiential and holistic: "Enacting the role and power of oral tradition and the strength of language is methodological in itself (as in Colorado, Deloria, Hermes and Young). Indigenous languages are descriptive and action or process oriented (Little Bear 2002). The awareness of Indigenous language and oral tradition causes a conscious searcher to attend to oral process" (2011: 90).

This book investigates the phenomenological perspective of the body, self and world as a philosophical tool towards understanding the diverse First Nations' folklore and worldview (as a complement to the emerging Indigenous scholarly discourse) from a non-dualistic, anti-rationalist and anti-Cartesian perspective. Therefore, the following discussion offers a critique of the Eurocentric dualisms — nature versus culture, self versus other, subject versus object, materiality versus spirituality and others — that contribute to the colonial disregard of First Nations' spiritual claims on their land. I explore the likelihood of a convergence between anti-rationalist, phenomenological trends in European thought with First Nations' stories and art works, which illustrate a holistic approach to the land's meaning as a spiritual continuum of body, self and world. I hope that employing such European philosophical concepts will make possible the creation of a non-ethnocentric niche within mainstream philosophical and litigious argumentation for the discussion of First Nations' land claims.

Since the time of Confederation, the provincial and federal governments have viewed the land's importance almost exclusively in utilitarian or economic terms, as is usual among European populations (Brody 1981). British Columbia First Nations are profoundly emotionally attached and "self-identified" with their respective territories. Thus, the land is supremely important to them, as they are now facing the courts with respect to the formalization of their constitutional, Aboriginal rights. First Nations within the Province of British Columbia are unique in that they were overlooked during the original federal treaty-making process, which took place during the consolidation of Canada's Confederation (Frideres and Gadacz 2005: 1889). At this time, most First Nations bands in Canada were allocated lands through this formal system. The treaty process moved westward across Canada but stopped at Treaty 8, which primarily exists in the province of Alberta but flows into the North Eastern corner of B.C.

Thus, British Columbia Native peoples have a long history of "struggle" which is qualitatively different than that of Native bands in other provinces. The distinguishing feature of B.C. First Nations' issues flow mainly from their exclusion from the treaty process. Due to the treaty-less state of First Nations within British Columbia (Frideres and Gadacz 2005: 189), there has been a longstanding need to uphold a comprehensive program of treaty-making throughout the province. Aboriginal and constitutional rights to land and resources, as enshrined in the 1982 Constitution of Canada, bear special significance for B.C.'s First Nations, whose legitimate claims to land were largely ignored in the original nation-building process. Since the time of Confederation, the First Nations within British Columbia have been fighting to have their Aboriginal rights upheld and have faced the growing problem of land shortage and overcrowding while living upon shrinking parcels of reserve land (Warry 2007). Thus, the courts now play a critical and challenging role in the arbitration of Aboriginal claims, in the ultimate shaping and re-figuring of Native identity and rights and in the process of de-colonization pursuant to the repatriation of the Canadian Constitution (Warry 2007).

Aboriginal and constitutional rights to land and resources, as enshrined in the Constitution of Canada, section 35, which was ratified April 17, 1982, have led to the Comprehensive Land Claims Policy of the Canadian government and to the British Columbia federal/provincial treaty process. The federal/provincial treaty process is a litigious process of land claims resolution, undertaken in consideration of section 35. Such governmental processes purport to demonstrate Canada's commitment to the resolution of Aboriginal land claims and constitutional rights. The alleged purpose of such "settlement agreements" is to provide certainty and clarity of rights to ownership and use of land and resources in those areas of Canada where Aboriginal title has not been dealt with by treaty, or been superseded by law. The Constitution, however, contains no clear-cut definition of the term "Aboriginal title." For First Nations peoples, Aboriginal title is inseparably bound with notions of sovereignty, self-determination and nationhood (Tennant 1990). The concept of sovereignty, as defined and espoused by Indigenous groups, implies that their people already have nationhood, dating back to the period before contact, and, therefore, the rights of both self-determination and self-government.

Recognition of sovereignty, through the settlement of claims based upon Aboriginal title, is a fundamental objective of B.C's Aboriginal people. The concept of First Nations' title and rights can be more fully grasped by looking at the unity of people and land, which informs Indigenous people's spirituality and worldview. First Nations people throughout British Columbia have always claimed a special connection and self-identification with their land and territory. Indeed, it is the basis of their Aboriginality, as shown in the following words by Indigenous scholar Richard Atleo: "As indicated earlier, reality is perceived as a unity: *heshook-is tswalk (nuu-chah-nulth)*. The physical spiritual realms are metaphorically connected and interrelated by the great waters" (2004: 17). First Nations in Canada argue that their special Aboriginal relationship to their own environments, traditional territories, ancestral traditions and cultures forms the basis of their Aboriginal rights and successful decolonization (Alfred 2009). According to Warry (2007: 30), "There is already a huge and objective body of social science research litera-ture that demonstrates that the solution to Aboriginal poverty, ill health, and marginalization — all the legacy of colonialism — lies in self-determination" — and thus the decolonization and restoration of Indigenous people to their own culture and ways (see also Armstrong 2000; Absolon 2011).

The structured relations of colonization must not be ignored with re-spect to Indigenous people's experiences. The homogenization of Native people into a single cultural entity in the *Indian Act* can be seen as an effort to eliminate First Nations under a federal program of assimilation into the "whitestream." In other words, it was an attempt at cultural genocide of the many distinct First Nations by a colonial presence imposing a Eurocentric settler-based hegemony (Warry 2007; Dickason 2006). As a result, many Indigenous people lost their identities and also their place within their own world, a condition which is frequently expressed through substance abuse, violence, criminalization and involvement with the child welfare system, as well as other behaviours associated with internalized oppression, coloniza-tion and poverty (Weaver 1990: 21). In the words of Dawn H., a Mohawk doctoral candidate from 1995: "Being a Native women, I also live with all the negative social problems associated with our people: high rates of alcoholism, violence, suicide, ill-heath, high mortality, poverty, and despair. They are not statistics to me. They are real — a part of me, my everyday life" (in Absolon 2011: 72). According to Dickason (2006: 271), "At the beginning of the twenty-first century, Aboriginal people were three times as likely to go to jail than non-Aboriginal people," a direct result of the dislocation felt by Indigenous people due to colonialism. In the words of renowned Native spokesperson Harold Cardinal, the *Indian Act* "subjugated to colonial rule the very people whose rights it was supposed to protect" (in Dickason 2006: 274).

According to Frideres and Gadacz, "Aboriginal people are in an identity crisis situation"; however, they "are beginning to have a clear vision of their own 'heritage' and culture, as distinguished from that of the 'mainstream' society" (2005: 16). For Cree Métis scholar Kathleen Absolon, First Nations' identity is locative, which means that locating oneself may come from a story, a narrative of our name, our family or one's history:

> Location links experiences of the self with experiences of others, facilitates connections and associations and heals relations.... Location varies from person to person, depending on our context. As we grow, change, learn and transform, how we locate changes. This is common because of our colonial history and experiences with residential schools and adoptions. (2011: 73)

Thus, clarifications of Indigenous identity have now become widespread and are rooted in a renewal of First Nations' forms of knowing, oral tradition and experience, and in a relocation of the Indigenous relation between self and other, and between the Indigenous self with the wider, external and surrounding world (Armstrong 2000; Absolon 2011).

The objective of this book is to re-open, within sociological discourse, the discussion of Native identity and meaning in British Columbia, in order to contribute to the on-going process of cultural recognition with respect to the importance of Indigenous "storyscapes" within tribal territories. I also hope that this work might add to a deepening of awareness for those working on First Nations' matters — especially with respect to those within the federal/provincial land claims processes — thereby adding to the appreciation for the culture and histories of the many unique First Nations cultures across British Columbia.

As noted, the subsumption of diverse Native cultures under one externally created term "Indian," to be administered under the *Indian Act*, became a form of cultural genocide designed to fast-track the federal government's agenda of assimilation of Aboriginal people to the white mainstream during the colonial period. The major challenge of the Canadian government now is one of how to "decolonize." This transition could prove to be painstaking as the Canadian justice system, which follows the thinking of the British system, prioritizes the goals of private property ownership and the rights of the individual. To date, the government has not provided a working framework for legitimating the many collectivist concerns of First Nations, whose histories are rooted in communal governance and possession, and who exercise Aboriginal tribal rights to collectively owned territories (McMillan and Yellowhorn 2004; Armstrong 1999). The utilitarian idea that everything in nature can be given a monetary value and that land and resources primarily have a material and economic value (the value of progress) is deeply ingrained within the Eurocentric consciousness of the mainstream. Moreover, the Canadian justice system and governmental system subscribe to this view. The realization that the value of the land for First Nations diverges sharply from this and is tied up with an entire way of existence, which is intrinsically a shared existence, is rarely considered.

First Nations' scholar, writer and educator Taiaiake Alfred (2009) expresses a view of de-colonization that decries all federal and court processes as colonial. He does not consider himself to be Canadian but to be a First Nations citizen within the borders of a nation the world recognizes as Canada. He argues that efforts to resolve First Nations' issues of culture, land and identity through discussions with the Canadian state (or through state processes) is non-Aboriginal in character, since the European model of governance differs vastly from that of First Nations, a problem which has never been addressed. Any attempt, therefore, on the part of First Nations to resolve questions of Aboriginal rights through the courts serves only to reproduce original models of colonialism and fosters an accompanying economic, political and ideological compliance on the part of First Nations peoples within their own national boundaries (Alfred 2009a). According to Absolon (2011: 101): "Decolonization is the common descriptor for unlearning racism and colonization and relearning and recovering Indigeneity."

At their core, European states and their colonial offspring still embody the same destructive and disrespectful impulses that they did two hundred years ago. Paulette Regan (2010: 6) states:

> Although the prime minister assured First Nations, Métis, and Inuit peoples that "there is no place in Canada for the attitudes that inspired the Indian residential school system to ever prevail again," my premise is that, unfortunately, such attitudes are still alive and well today, rooted in settler historical myths and colonial mindsets. To understand why this is, it is instructive to explore how colonial violence is woven into the fabric of Canadian history in an unbroken thread from past to present, which we must now unravel, upsetting our comfortable assumptions about the past. At the same time, we must work as Indigenous allies to "restory" the dominant-culture version of history; that is, we must make decolonizing space for Indigenous history-counter-narratives of diplomacy, law and peacemaking practices-as told by Indigenous peoples themselves.

For this reason, questions of justice — social, political and environmental — are best considered outside the framework of classical European thought and legal traditions. The value of breaking away from old patterns of thought and developing innovative responses has been demonstrated with respect to environmental questions. According to Kathleen Absolon: "The stories are limited in their presentation because so much time has to be spent countering eurowestern hegemonies" (2011: 101). But, in fact, many of these and other pressing questions have been answered before: Indigenous traditions are the repository of vast experience and deep insight on achieving balance and harmony.

According to Sorflaten and Smith, research, methodology, theory and action are complex issues for Indigenous scholars (and for those within First Nations communities) because what passes for knowledge within modern society is part of the colonial enterprise; it is thus heavily steeped in Western, Eurocentric approaches (Smith, in Sorflaten 2006) The two systems of knowledge — colonial versus First Nations — cannot be conflated. Armstrong asserts that Indigenous people's rights are "really not just theory. People are suffering worldwide. Indigenous people are suffering the worst.... You cannot just talk about it. You have to do things about it" (2000: 144–45). In Armstrong's story *Whispering from the Shadows*, her character Penny has a worldview deeply rooted in "local consciousness" (41), which Armstrong argues to be indispensably necessary for any sort of resistance movement. According to Armstrong, "Aboriginal community, then, is about family, yet it is more than just family it is a thing deeper and more enduring than any one of us" (273; see also Sorflaten 2006).

The Threefold Structure of Enfoldment, Storyscape and *Poiesis*

In keeping with the arguments above, a worldview beyond dualistic thinking presents me with an interactive environment which is a part of me and which is "enfolded" into the fabric of my own body as my own experience of my skin. Thus, with non-dualism, the notion of self is not an individual self but a collective self which encompasses all of my experiences within a given context of terrestrial social action, which in the case of First Nations can be explained as the tribal territory. The perception of the land as an entire way of life looms large for the many treatyless First Nations within British Columbia and, for First Nations, takes precedence over the economic viewpoint. The experience of the land as an enfoldment of all people's experiences and stories gives rise to the realization that the land is inseparably connected to personhood — not simply inert or external to personal identity and being. Identity rather is a regional and territorial matter that speaks to human experiences — on the land, within a particular cultural, linguistic and geographic niche — and therefore, is specific to a distinct group of territorial dwellers rather than being homogeneous across First Nations. Because the territory is not ontologically separate from humans in the case of the

First Nations' stories under study, the land and the features of the territory are noticeably animate, have personhood and are meaningful and spiritual. In fact, it is this land-based spirituality, this territorial significance, plus a place-related experience of being (set within the terrestrial surroundings), that inheres within the First Nations' oral traditions and "storyscapes" and that gives testimony to an Aboriginal selfhood. It is through the corporal experience of the extended body, with respect to being-on-the-land, that First Nations have become deeply self-identified with their territories over multiple generations and thus experience it as part of their own skin and, in some cases, as a part of their own family. The understanding of the territory as a lived human story, or "storyscape" (within a regional landscape), speaks to the question of identity and human meaning and to the emotional and spiritual value of land, as it is lived and spoken. This is in contrast to a Eurocentric, universal, economic, utilitarian model of the land's value, private property and economic ownership, which characterize the legal political discourses in Canada.

In the words of Cree scholar Kathleen Absolon:

> Doing and being creative are operative here. There comes a point in our process when we need to go beyond the writing and move from the cerebral, heart and Spirit into the doing and being (Rice 2003). Words alone are not enough in a culture that is experiential, holistic, land based and connected to all of Creation. (Absolon 2011: 132)

Thus, the tribal territory (or the field of tribal activity and Aboriginal selfhood) can be described as giving rise to poetic expressions, or in other words to a "poetics of existence" — a *poiesis* — that emerges out of the people's terrestrial experiences and manifests as their oral traditions, their stories, their artworks, their songs and their dances. As per European phenomenology, the consequence of a non-Cartesian imbrication of people and land is the occurrence of a territorial speaking, in poetic and expressive terms, through the spiritual and emotive gestures of the people from their extended territorial body.

"The grammar of aboriginal hopes and fears," writes Edward Chamberlin, "the logic that informs their stories and songs, is a spiritual grammar; it's not a social or economic or political or even a cultural one"[3] (in Gill 2009: 139). According to Entriken, a crisis within modernity and the understanding of indigeneity involves a gap in consciousness between a relatively objective point of view and a relatively subjective point of view--as found in the existing tensions between tradition and modernity's empirical and utilitarian focus.

A *poiesis* of being and doing (as an active emergence of the self's expression) ultimately speaks to the people's being-on-the-land collectively and to the land's meaning as a spiritual value, as well as to a community personality in both aesthetic and moral terms. Such a *poiesis* also communicates the experiential and emotive nexus of the people in the land and of the land in the people and to the realization of all of their experiences of life. A *poiesis* of people and land by necessity speaks to the matter of First Nations' identity and collective selfhood, since the cultural/aesthetic expressions occurring within a given First Nation emerge out of an experience of enfoldment with their territorial environment, as their own extended body. The oral traditions and poetic/aesthetic moments arising from the territory demonstrate the spiritual and emotional affiliations of the people as situated.

Thus, the *poiesis* (the aesthetic or symbolic moments that characterize the culture) are embedded within the storied landscape, or "storyscape," which geographically anchors each culturally distinct First Nation as separate, in contrast to the colonial homogenization under the *Indian Act*. The storyscape that maps out the dimensions of the territory and that speaks to the moral and cultural definition of the territorial people and their collective selfhood refutes the colonial notion of ethnic sameness (across the many diverse First Nations groups). Therefore, all the aesthetic representations within the territory bear witness to the enfoldment of people and land as a non-Cartesian value. A territorial poetics, as can be seen in First Nations within British Columbia, can be found in the many mythological landmarks, in Transformer stones as given in creation stories, in masks for coastal peoples, in special places on the land such as power spots, in songs, in the oral traditions, in the language, in the dances and in many other forms. Thus, the concept of "storyscape" (Stoffle, Halmo and Austin 1995) represents the collective story of a given First Nation, which anchors people on the land meaningfully in the way that makes it an ancestral "dwelling," because it ties people together on the land as part of a collective moral and practical system. Such a system is implied, for example, in the Okanagan term *en'owkin*, explained by Okanagan First Nation scholar Jeannette Armstrong (1999) as the natural process of survival that includes the entire community, the traditional knowledge and the land.

What we refer to as a storyscape, as it exists on the land, is able to instruct, guide and teach the people within their own collective ancestral and terrestrial background. At each moment, the storyscape expresses the collective enfoldment of people and land with the surrounding animals and with each other as a totality in the non-dualistic sense (Elsey 2001; Cove 1987a; Scott 1989). The poetics of place, referred to here as *poiesis*, conceptualizes the many aesthetic values (such as mythic landmarks, songs, dances, stories etc.) present within the territory, as they are orally encoded and animated by narratives within the wider storyscape, which is geographical in its dimensions. Such aesthetic movements serve to demarcate and anchor the human space as a meaningful human dwelling (Armstrong, in Jensen 2004; Heidegger 1971a).

It is these poetic and artistic moments of human expression that speak to people's feelings and experiences as they are lived and which simultaneously map and establish the world as a culturally defined and meaningful human space (Heidegger 1971a). It is the *poiesis* of land and human activity that expresses the meaningfulness of the journeys of humans (as the movements of the lived body in space) and creates a storied landscape that anchors the culture according to the territorial meanings, its spirituality and its art. Therefore, because the land is the repository and archive of such deep social and ecological meanings and records people's actual journeys and life experiences, it is realistic to make the claim that the land is in the people as much as the people are in the land (Abram 1996). As such, the identity and meaning of the Aboriginal peoples is inscribed in the territory, where it is expressed both narratively and artistically. It is for this reason that the people are integrally and inseparably self-identified with their territory.

These sentiments are summed up by Atleo in his comments about his grandmother:

> When I became a young man and was able to go off by myself into the great world, my grandmother Margaret would always say to me as I left: *"Tloo-utl-ee-sum."* At that time I did not understand why she would want me to remember her in my travels. Now, in my later years, I can see the great theme that remembrance plays in the drama of life among the Nuu-chah-nulth. Every great ceremony demanded remembrances of who owned what, who had what name, who owned this dance and that song, who owned this *tupati* (spiritual power), where *hahuulti* (ancestral territory) came from, and what we must do each day upon awakening: namely, remember Qua-ootz, Owner of All That Is, Owner of Reality. In your travels into different languages and cultures, remember me; don't forget where you came from; remember your roots, your rich heritage. (2004: 95)

The Rationale

The intrinsic value of each individual First Nation as a storyscape is critical within British Columbia at this time because the Canadian state is currently involved in a constitutional process of re-shaping cultural identity markers and economic boundaries for First Nations people through the federal/provincial treaty process. After at least three ground-breaking cases — *Nisga'a*, *Sparrow* and *Gitxan/Wet'suwet'en* (Frideres and Gadacz 2005) — and Supreme Court decisions on Aboriginal rights, both federal and provincial levels of government have to face the legitimacy of native claims.[4] Nevertheless, the constitutional process that has emerged seems to speak neither to the genuine Aboriginal heritages nor to an experiential Aboriginality (Mills 2005;

Culhane 1998). In other words, the criteria of Aboriginal rights and title required by the Canadian courts during land claims cases does not reflect an authentic First Nations way of life as it is experienced in the First Nations communities or on the land, as explained by Indigenous peoples living in their traditional territories in British Columbia. Kathleen Absolon argues for the validation and greater centrality of First Nations' intellectual traditions when she states: "Charging that mainstream historical literature 'imprisons Indian history' through the silencing of Indigenous perspectives and voices, and 'by the rhetoric and scholarly inventions of empire' Native American scholars argue for a new articulation of Indigenous scholarship grounded in tribal intellectual traditions" (2011: 101).

In fact, it is still largely the case that ethnocentric and hegemonic epistemologies within Canadian institutions (such as the courts) have never been properly addressed (Alfred 2009a). For example, Armstrong suggests it is important to track the local toward a "breaking with the illusion of Western development and progress as a world order" (in Sorflaten 2006). Such a process of illumination of the "local over the global," according to Armstrong, would highlight the space of global disorientation and challenge the universality of Western epistemology or worldview as the standard order and dominant knowledge form (Sorflaten 2006).

In truth, the threat of widespread assimilation of Indigenous people in British Columbia and across Canada is far from over. For example, it has been argued by conservative scholars, and in the context of Canadian courts, that First Nations peoples' adoption of modern technology indicates their accomplished assimilation into the mainstream, whereas concomitantly, First Nations' meaning of territory is frequently lost in crosscultural translation — threatening First Nations (whose claims are under review) with new forms of colonization (see Mills 2005; Warry 2007). However, Wayne Warry, among others demonstrates that, far from representing Westernization, the adoption of modern technologies has taken place in the context of First Peoples' unique worldviews and cultural ways: "It has become apparent that Aboriginal people, rather than *adopting* Western practices and ideas, were adapting them to suit their own cultural purposes" (Warry 2007: 35). Thus, Aboriginal peoples in Canada, and elsewhere, are involved in a foot race: to preserve their cultural knowledge and local, geographic identity before time and assimilationist policies erase the historical threads to their immediate and practising pasts.

Not only does the cultural and spiritual identity of First Nations peoples hang in the balance, but the community and land-based existence of these peoples is at risk, requiring the garnering of enough "cultural identifiers" to give concrete empirical and legal evidence to the courts regarding the First Nations' self-identification with place. As I demonstrate below, the land itself (the storyscape) can stand as a text when serious consideration is given to First Nations' stories and oral accounts. The designation of a cultural conflict between traditions versus modernity, with respect to subjective-versus-objective points of view (Entriken 1991; Couture 1991), offers a reference point for the importance of story as a method of cutting through ethnocentric, Eurocentric texts in the context of the court room. As shown through many examples in Chapters 4, 5 and 6, it is the land that has guided people's terrestrial actions and understandings. Thus, the land itself, or the storyscapes, can provide the cultural identifiers of longstanding First Nations' attachment to place.

Often, understandings about another party's use patterns within a common landscape are represented within a body of folklore subscribed to by two or more tribal groups, as is largely the case, for example, with the Secwepemc and the Nlaka pamux (Teit 1912b, 1909). Such ancestral Aboriginal practices and the reality of these storyscapes are at odds with a Eurocentric commitment to "hard" evidence and utilitarian values, as presented in the interpretive frameworks established by the courts, pursuant to section 35 of the 1982 *Constitution Act*. As Russ Hoffman demonstrates in "The Legacy of Joe Couture's Work within the Discipline of Native Studies" (2011), the Aboriginal teacher and scholar Joe Couture argues for the importance of subjectivism and oral tradition and story in the understanding of First Nations' life-ways of all kinds and as necessary to consider in First Nations' scholarship. Couture's work emphasizes that Eurocentric academia is anathema to "Native knowing," and he stresses the central importance of oral literature when considering any kind of Indigenous knowledge or meaning.

Couture (1991: 68) tells us: "Oral literature is and must be considered as a medium in its own right, apart from textuality, if one wants to study Indigenous knowledge. That is a starting point or requirement." He elaborates that the "traditional indigenous mind is an oral literature dependent mind" (58). Thus, the main objective of this book is to demonstrate that the First Nations peoples of British Columbia live within what can be described as storyscapes, which are recorded and passed along orally and which should be used as primary evidence in the resolution of all Indigenous claims. Such stories reflect the activities, feelings and memories of the people within a given place and map out the dimensions of the territory as a field of age-old human activity and human use. The storyscapes can be seen as poetically defined cultural landscapes that are anchored by aesthetic or artistic moments that speak to the meaningfulness of the land and territory within the identity of the local people. The many artistic and poetic expressions of territorial existence nested within storyscapes speak non-dualistically to the people's experiences in practical, affective and spiritual terms. In the absence of Cartesian modes of thinking, their surrounding territory is tantamount to the people's experience of their own skin as they are enfolded with it in their "ownmost" experience of identity. As such, the tribal territories of First Nations within British Columbia must be seen as inalienable as they carry a meaning that is clearly not measurable or calculable in economic terms.

Although section 35 of the repatriated Canadian Constitution appears to support de-colonization through a re-instatement of outstanding Aboriginal rights, Aboriginal rights are actually at odds with the Eurocentric commitment to statistical evidence and utilitarian values, which are alive and well in the new legislative and interpretive frameworks pursuant to section 35. To further de-colonize and to avoid further assimilation, the importance of land as an existential framework — not just an economic framework — must be taken seriously. That way, the inseparability of the land from the people (as one united process of being and doing) will come sharply into view, and the uniqueness of each First Nation as a continuous historical entity, as a language group, as a territorial entity and as a specific cultural people will no longer be overlooked. For over a century, the First Nations within British Columbia have been made invisible (Regan 2010) as a result of a colonial presence that placed them under the *Indian Act* in an attempt to subsume each distinct First Nation under one imaginary and undivided ethnicity. As a result, each nation started to cede from public view; each storyscape and language was placed seriously in jeopardy. Over time, under the sway of the federal government's assimilation policy,[5] — including the residential schools, potlatch legislation, the enfranchisement program, and other forms of cultural genocide — the ways of the people within each territory became largely invisible.

According to Warry (2007), the *Indian Act* is an antiquated legislative tool to bring about assimilation of First Nations into the mainstream. Many government policies and practices were aimed at encouraging or forcing Aboriginal people to assimilate in order to rid Canada of the so-called Indian problem (37). "The Indian Act (1876) consolidated many prior pieces of legislation and still governs the state's relationship to Aboriginal peoples today."[6]

Paulette Regan, in her book *Unsettling the Settler Within: Indian Residential Schools, Truth Telling, and Reconciliation in Canada* (2010), tells us about the invisibility of Indigenous peoples to other Canadians throughout three generations of residential schooling, with the last school closing down as late as 1996. Regan discloses predominant myths of the Canadian mainstream by studying a journey of survivors to recovery from their harrowing residential school experiences[7]:

> The schools, some of which are still standing, remain comfortably invisible to Canadians as do the former inhabitants themselves.... What does the persistence of such invisibility in the face of the living presence of survivors tell us about our relationship with Indigenous

peoples? What does our historical amnesia reveal about our continuing complicity in denying, erasing and forgetting this part of our history as colonizers while pathologizing the colonized? (Regan 2010: 6)

According to Alfred, Warry, Tennant and Asch et al., Aboriginal leaders in Canada call for an end of discrimination policies and the creation of
a viable land base, which could pave the way to self-government for First
Nations. For example, Warry states: "Despite failed government policy and
the marginal economic status of reserves, land is essential to Aboriginal
identity, and a sustainable land base an essential component of Aboriginal
self-government" (2007: 40).

Yet another phenomenon of colonization and assimilation which must
be evaluated in the quest for de-colonization and re-storying was that each
First Nation's living territorial map was covered over by a non-Aboriginal
map showing places, boundaries and regions devised by the Canadian state
or the provinces. Such maps do not reflect the use and life patterns of First
Nations' communities (Brody 1981). The way to guarantee the Aboriginal
rights of the many distinct First Nations within British Columbia is to bring
them squarely into public view and to overcome appropriation of voice
and years of legal and bureaucratic precedent that stands between the First
Nations people and their Aboriginal rights determination. The acknowledge-
ment of each territorial group as a narrative entity (Armstrong 1999) that
can only be understood through their own local and collective story can lead
us to a sincere legitimation of Native claims.

In the current phase of "world globalism," NAFTA and a world order
of economic centralization, there is an increasing need to resist new forms
of economic and cultural assimilation of Indigenous peoples (Hall 1997:
173–87) and to emphasize the local over the global in preventing First Nations
homogenization. Decolonization of Indigenous people, both in Canada
and abroad, is under constant threat from new forms of re-colonization
at both the global and national levels (within their surrounding nation
states). According to Armstrong (2000), Hall (1997) and Sorflaten (2006)
et al., there is a significant danger of Indigenous homogenization through
global mass economic culture, which both includes but also transcends the
boundaries of national state governments (see also Comaroff and Comaroff
2009). Dirlik (1996) argues that recent decades have seen a proliferation of
local movements as "the primary if not the only expression of resistance to
domination." Maracle (1990), Smith (1999), Ruffo (1999) and Dirlik (1999)
write on the importance of the Aboriginal locale as a site of resistance to
capital which offers space for local imagining for non-assimilated futures
and Indigenous possibility. Jeannette Armstrong (1999b) examines her
character Penny's resistance to globalization through her art and activism

as a method of returning to Indigenous localism and preserving Indigenous difference in the global epoch. For Heike Harting (2004), "globetrotting" is a transnational economic trope which attempts the further dispossession of Indigenous peoples, along with the development and accelerated exploitation of Indigenous lands under the auspices of progress and neoliberal rhetoric, falsely recoded as the bringer of universal economic improvement. The concept of spiritual grammar as resistance is captured in Gill's discussions with Haida orator and carver Guujaw, "whose constant references to the land, and the supernatural, is a constant manifestation of resistance" (Gill 2009: 137). For Edward Chamberlain, Indigenous spiritual grammar "is grounded in a knowledge and belief in something beyond easy understanding, expressed in the stories and songs as well as the dances and paintings that speak about the spirits. And it pushes back against both the pressure of reality and the pressure of other people's imaginations. It is a blockade too, saying no to other ways of being-in-the-world" (in Gill 2009: 139).

Increasingly, critics of globalization, such as Frank Davey and Herb Wylie, hold up regionalism as a political strategy in support of cultural sites of resistance to homogenizing and widespread global assumptions. The hope of reconstructing First Nations' differences as multifaceted, subjective and complex, with respect to the local (and to the global) offers the possibility of writing against essentialist notions of aboriginality and thus against homogenizing tropes of First Nations' identities (Sorflaten 2006; Clifford and Marcus 1986). Due to pressures from colonization and the resultant poverty of Indigenous peoples, it is not surprising that there has been a large egress of Indigenous people to the urban areas in Canada. "Like many people from all backgrounds, the migration has been generated because jobs tend to be in the urban areas, thus over one-half of Aboriginal people live in urban areas. Many reserves are in rural and isolated areas with high unemployment or poor infrastructure" (Sorflaten 2006). According to Silver (2008) Aboriginals in the cities "face a host of difficulties — inadequate housing, shortage of work, unsafe neighbourhoods, racism in various forms... higher rates of unemployment, a higher incidence of poverty and lower levels of income, on the average, than do non-Aboriginal people" (Rodriguez (11) in Honoré, McCormick and Carmen 2006).

Nevertheless, Indigenous identity, spirituality and culture are equally important for Indigenous people in urban areas as for those in rural areas. Many urban First Nations place an equal importance of land and story as do their rural counterparts. Thus, while I strongly acknowledge the importance of meaning and identity for all Indigenous people, both rural and urban, it is beyond the scope of this book to deal with the specific topics of urbanized indigeneity. This book focuses largely on the importance of land and story as a site of Indigenous legitimation, resistance and identity for the many First Nations and their diverse traditional territories throughout British Columbia. While its research base is predominantly regions outside of the heavily urbanized areas of British Columbia, I do not differentiate between rural versus urban Indigenous peoples with respect to the topic at hand. Even in Greater Vancouver, First Nations such as the Tsleil-Waututh, Squamish, Musqueam, Stó:lō and others have an abiding and active interest in their natural, spiritual and sensitive areas as active Aboriginal claims (Carleson 1997, 2010; Carlson, McHalsie and Shaepe 2001; Reimer 2000, 2003; Squamish Nation 2012; Tsleil-Waututh 2012; Musqueam Nation 2012). The Musqueam state on their website: "Although a metropolitan city has developed in the heart of *Musqueam* territory, our community maintains strong cultural and traditional beliefs. Our community historians and educators teach and pass on our history to our people, which has always been the way of our people, to keep our culture and traditions strong."

Chapters 4, 5 and 6 offer an overview of ethnographic studies of First Nations peoples, assembling a collection of voices and thus providing local meanings through First Nations people's own oral and written accounts. Throughout this book, I present writings and quotations offered by First Nations people, wherever possible drawing on the oral words of the people themselves, as they have been recorded within the existing published ethnographic record. It is not the intention of this book to provide any kind of formula for Indigenous methodology or claim that its pages are representative of Indigenous methodology or research. I hope that the study might serve to help non-Indigenous scholars, researchers, consultants and others who are engaged in Aboriginal work, to find a deeper understanding of the non-dualistic Indigenous approaches to land, territory and story, thus to problematize Eurocentric and utilitarian approaches to the topic of Aboriginal land.

Chapter 2 offers a brief history of the Aboriginal rights struggle in British Columbia and situates the problematic of de-colonization and the role of governments and constitutional policy with respect to the concerns of First Nations peoples. The chapter analyzes First Nations' identity and the land question and problematizes statist methods of establishing Aboriginal rights through litigious criteria that frustrate the process of decolonization of First Nations within Canada. I argue that requiring First Nations to prove their Aboriginal rights to the satisfaction of the courts through the presentation of hard evidence is tendentious in that it serves mainstream utilitarian " assimilationist approaches (already in sway under the *Indian Act*). By placing First Nations peoples at risk of co-optation to the agendas of government and to the utilitarian methods of the mainstream, First Nations' self-determination, regional and community-based will, and Indigenous identity are at risk. First Nations' identity is argued to be community-based and territorial as opposed to state-fostered. The book's position of a land-based poetics (as given in

Chapter 1) that originates in First Nations' oral traditions and storyscapes, is applied as a rebuttal to current litigious methods of proving and establishing Aboriginal rights through court precedents and empirical tests.

In Chapter 3, The conceptualization of the concepts of *"poiesis"* and "storyscape" is developed to demonstrate how First Nations peoples are experientially enfolded within their traditional territories emotively, aesthetically, spiritually and activationally in ways that are central to the formation of the Indigenous self. The concept of *poiesis* is elaborated from the theories of European phenomenology (as offered in the works of Martin Heidegger, Maurice Merleau-Ponty and others[8]) in order to open up a philosophical discourse (with the use of a non-Cartesian western philosophical tradition) that can contribute to a better understanding of the self-identification and corporeal imbrication with which First Nations people relate to their ancestral surroundings.

Chapter looks at the storyscapes of certain coastal First Nations through the application of the phenomenological concepts of body, self and world with respect to coastal peoples. Drawing on the existing ethnographic record, this chapter examines the presence of *poiesis* for various coastal First Nations and demonstrates the importance of aesthetic forms such as stories, songs, dances, masks and crests in forming the land-based identity of Indigenous peoples who live and work within their ancestral territories. The chapter provides a phenomenological analysis of aspects of the Stó:lō, Gitxan, Nisga'a, Kwakwakawakw, Nuu-chah-nulth and Taku River Tlingit traditions and systems of land tenure and social organization, in terms of *poiesis* and enfoldment of self, body and world. This chapter demonstrates how the people are in the land as much as the land is in the people, thus giving the territory animate meaning and "personhood."

Chapter 5 provides a phenomenological discussion on the storyscapes present in the interior of British Columbia, within what is referred to as the plateau culture area. The chapter looks at Transformer stories from both the Statliumx and Nlaka'pamux peoples while investigating the presence of mythological landmarks as *poiesis*, thus situating the stories and landmarks within territorial watersheds as age-old regions of Aboriginal activity. The Lillooet River stories with respect to a specific "territorial watershed" or "regional landscape" are analyzed and presented as examples of storyscapes that spell out a First Nation's activity. The upper Statliumx storyscape embraces their creation stories as a *poiesis* of people and land. Through the poetic storied landmarks of the Nlaka'pamux, we see how the journeys of Transformer deities map the land for human habitation.

In Chapter 6, the Nlaka'pamux Stein Valley serves as a regional storyscape where the experience of an Indigenous "environmental" surrounding is discoverable in a wide variety of expressive and iconic forms that speak to the *poiesis* of body and world. Thus, the many cultural depictions found within the Stein Valley serve to illustrate the epidermis between the people and the surrounding valley as their own skin. The ethnographic research presented within the chapter demonstrates how regional landscapes are features within the self's *poiesis* and how they provide an analysis of storyscapes as environmentally inalienable Indigenous landscapes.

Chapter 7 summarizes the book through philosophical, historical and ethnographic discussions that demonstrate the necessity of applying a non-Cartesian approach to the land's importance within First Nations' territories. The chapter provides an overview of the book's arguments and demonstrates, through problematizing Occidental categories, why the phenomenological concepts of "enfoldment," "storyscape" and "*poiesis*" are helpful for the intellectual work of de-colonization and for explaining the requirement of genuine Indigenous voice.

Notes

1. The Britany Triangle is the traditional territory of the Xeni Gwet'in people of the Chilcotin region of British Columbia. The Xeni Gwet'in is a First Nations band within the Tsilhgot'in language group whose territory is situated near to the modern town of Williams Lake.

2. The "Opinion Area" in the Xeni Gwet'in land claim case, is an area used and claimed by the Xeni *Gwet'in Tsilhgot'in,* but which Justice Vickers referred back to a higher court for further negotiation. This "opinion area" was claimed by Xeni Gwet'in, but not included in the claim, in Justice Vickers' original claim area.

3. Thus, Sorflaten cites Dirlik, Hall, Wilson and Dissanayake on the importance of "local knowledge," along with Maracle, Smith, Ruffo to emphasize the importance of the Indigenous locale — as a site for imagining future alternatives and thus sites of hope and resistance.

4. Section 35 in the Canadian Constitution was left vague in its explanation of Aboriginal rights, although they were acknowledged. Thus, Aboriginal rights in Canada has been tried through a number of court cases that have been president setting, the most important of which are *Calder vs. the Queen, Sparrow vs. the Queen, Vanderpeet vs. the Queen,* the *Delgamuukw* Decision (of the Gitxan and Wet'suwet'en) and the Xeni Gwet'in Tsilhgot'in land claim judgment.

5. The federal government's original intentions for Canada's Indigenous peoples were the ultimate dissolution of the tribes and nations and their eventual absorption, or assimilation, to the mainstream society. The government of Canada systematically created legislation to accomplish this objective.

6. The "Enfranchisement Policy" under the *Indian Act* (the trading of Indian status for full Canadian citizenship) was the most obvious technique of the government's attempts at assimilation. However the requirement of loss of status for Aboriginal women who married non-Native men was another attempt to stimulate assimilation through inter-marriage and through the loss of Indian status of Aboriginal women (and her children). This policy was eliminated in

1986 with the passing of Bill C-31 and Bill C-3, which were passed to eliminate the extant sexism inherent in the *Indian Act*.

7.   Throughout the book, she gives testimony to the deep-seated psychological and physical wounds incurred by First Nations residential school students, who were forced to attend these schools over several generations, while the majority of Canadians were largely ignorant that the schools even existed.

8.   Martin Heidegger and Maurice Merleau-Ponty were both European philosophers who developed the discourse of phenomenology to overcome the intellectual hegemony of enlightenment thinkers such as Rene Descartes, who argued that scientific rationalism is the superior academic method for understanding the physical world.

Chapter 2

First Nations' Identity
through a History of Struggle

My "Nativeness" is based on lineage, cultural affiliation, my personal beliefs, values and spiritual relationship to the word "Native." (Laura Schwager 2003)

Since the initiation of the federal *Indian Act* of 1876, the history of First Nations in British Columbia has been one of political struggle, imposed colonial identity, language loss, homogenization and the breakdown of self-government and livelihood (Frideres and Gadacz 2005: 23). As the traditional identity of the First Nations in British Columbia, like that of all hunter-gatherers, is largely directed towards the land, the fact that their ancestral land rights, since the time of Canada's Confederation, have not been legally acknowledged by all levels of government has been particularly troubling. The Aboriginal identity of the First Nations people in Canada has always been one of unbroken relatedness to the land[1] through an embodied and community-based meaning system of respect, in direct contrast to European models of rationalistic, Cartesian, individualistic humans. The belief that humans had a spiritual connection to the land necessitated that they assume a special role as stewards with respect to it. First Nations' oral traditions, creation stories and storyscapes told them that they were situated within their territories by the Creator and thus have a divinely inspired but natural role within it. According to Kahnawake Mohawk scholar and teacher Taiaiake Alfred (2006), nowhere is the contrast between the colonists and the traditional Aboriginal in Canada more noticeable and pronounced than in First Nations' ancestral philosophy about land and territory. Whereas Western viewpoints on the earth tend to be governed by the forces of capital and economic gain (utilitarian approach), "Indigenous philosophies are premised on the belief that earth was created by a power external to human beings, who have a responsibility to act as stewards; since humans had no hand in making the earth, they had no right to possess it or dispose of it as they see fit - possession of land and humankind is unnatural and unjust" (327).

A widescale globalization of lands and resources is remote from Indigenous methods of stewardship, spirituality and responsibility, which incorporate the unity of land and story and in which care of the land is both a familial and local responsibility, as shown by Jeanette Armstrong (1999) in "Let Us Begin With Courage." According to Harting (2004: 262), "globalization connives and plots narratives of deliberate social and economic underdevelopment and reinvents itself as the sign and carrier of the good and just society," while Armstrong explains that globalization and conceptions of the new world order challenge the Indigenous peoples being incorporated into the world's marketplace, thus demanding forms of resistance (in Sorflaten 2006).

First Nations scholars Alfred, Armstrong and Atleo argue that life on the land is tied to the existence of stories, traditional knowledge and customs and is viewed as a spiritual concern — which involves the notion of care and respect — on the part of all humans towards each other and also towards the other ecological features of the territory (including the plant and animal people and the landscape, which also is animated and has personhood). Thus, it can be argued that First Nations people are self-identified with and live their lives within spiritual and moral universes (or storyscapes) that maintain a holistic and spiritual relationship between the people and the land, which has inculcated an attitude of care. The origin stories of virtually all First Nations peoples throughout British Columbia describe the tribes and clans as descended from the territory's plant and animal beings, or as related to special geological landmarks. It is the artistic and poetical customs, the dances, songs and stories, that have always taught people how to care for the land and each other and that have passed on the unique worldview and identity which insures the survival of each tribe (Cove 1987a; Cruikshank 1990; Atleo 2004). Thus, First Nations scholars, Alfred, Armstrong and others have called for the revitalization of traditionalism, which revives the telling of stories and a return to many of the old customs, like the tribal circles and the longhouse ceremonies. Native people threaten their survival when they frame their struggle for Aboriginal identity and for land claims against the sovereignty of the state. In the eyes of the hegemonic state, Aboriginal people have no role in the new myths except as either enemies or a dying race. "The struggle for justice would be better served by undermining the myth of state sovereignty then, by carving out a small and dependent space for Indigenous peoples within it... So I think we should institute new customs, and have some nights set aside to do storytelling... We should also teach the old clan and kinship responsibilities, and make deliberate efforts to carry them out" (Korsmo in Alfred 2009b: 82).

Nuu-chah-nulth scholar Richard Atleo offers the idea that modern society could not get started until people gave up all of their stories and tales, or that modern society actually began with "the leaving off of tales" (Atleo 2004; see also Web 1959). Thus, the turning away from tales issued in the dawning of the scientific age and, along with it, the advent of so-called modern persons with all the classifications and dualities that accompanied that transition. With this step, the many dualities typical of the Cartesian human could arise, starting with the separation of subject and object, which results in the alienation of humans from the rest from nature (as something material and external to humans), and the separation of self versus other (as in the modern individual); both of which contravene the experience of holism as traditionally lived within First Nation's communities (Couture 1991; Armstrong 1999; Absolon 2011; Baskin 2006).

> Oral tradition should be a central concern.... But that requires faculty members that have a developed sense of oral tradition and a prolonged experience in ceremonies. That challenge is in turn compounded by traditional university intellectualism vs. Native intuition; of academics vs. colloquial languages; of elitism vs. people in communities; of knowledge of the professional vs. direct knowledge; and of written tradition vs. oral tradition. (Couture 1991: 65)

As shown in Hugh Brody's well-known book *Maps and Dreams* (1981), Aboriginal identity (in Northern British Columbia, for example) has evolved as life lived within a territory, as life in families, lineages and hunting bands, and through responding to the cyclical processes of nature as necessitated by the seasonal harvesting of wild plants and animals (see also Ingold 1996; Hudson 2006). Life on the land, therefore, implies a life meshed with the seasons, with the migration of animals and fish and which is flexible to the harshness of the elements throughout the course of the year. Consequently, traditional First Nations' life has been lived inseparable from nature, which required consideration of all of its nuances and therefore a profound respect for sustainability. Okanagan scholar Jeanette Armstrong explains community decision-making as a political method of sustainability and survival that engages the whole community together with the land. However, as yet, Native identity as an "embodied identity," as a communal life on the land which incorporates lineage and cultural affiliation and a land-based spirituality, has never been appreciated in colonial definitions of Aboriginal rights. As a case in point, the Okanagan term *en'owkin* frames an approach to speaking about the land as part of worldview and family, as inseparable from the Okanagan people themselves and as integral to their community-based decision-making (Armstrong 1999).

Consideration of First Nations' identity as one of difference, as one that is enfolded within the territory and integrated within a community and passed-on through the stories and local customs of the tribe, is absent in the governing objectives and constitutional discourses which inform section 35 of the Canadian *Constitution Act*. Government policy in Canada, pursuant to two constitutions for over a century, has focused on both the control and the extinction of the diverse First Nations' cultures across Canada and on the assertion of Canadian sovereignty (Frideres and Gadacz 2005: 2; Alfred 2009a). Moreover, the *British North America Act* and the federal *Indian Act* do not give consideration to the First Nations peoples' cultural and spiritual identity and do not support the differences between First Nations' values versus colonial ones.

In the eyes of anyone opposed to historical and modern-day colonization,

> Indian status was and is a fictitious creation, used to manipulate Native people, to destabilize First Nations, and to co-opt their lands and resources. To believe in the Indian Act definitions of identity prevents many Native people from knowing and owning their culture. They allow their identity to be determined by a piece of paper, and their culture to be controlled by a law vastly removed from any of their traditional values. They allow for their extinction. And yet we are here. The drum keeps beating. (Schwager 2003: 52)

The Land Question

The land problem, and the related problem of lost or homogenized identity, that characterizes all First Nations people living under the *Indian Act* throughout Canada has been particularly intense in British Columbia. Although disenfranchisement under the *Indian Act* was the same for the First Nations in British Columbia, their history is in many ways dissimilar to the majority of other Canadian tribes. While the tribes in the rest of Canada received treaties as the provinces entered into Confederation, the government of British Columbia abstained from land surrenders to Native peoples, contrary to Ottawa's recommendation that they should reach settlements with First Nations. In many ways, the departure on the part of B.C. from precedents in the rest of Canada set the stage for a more protracted history of political struggle and greater hardship among the First Nations within B.C.

Although treaties across the rest of Canada were often inadequate and are due for renegotiation,[2] British Columbia's First Nations' land problem is unique due to the historical absence of treaties, with the exception of a few small ones that were signed with Native groups on Vancouver Island when British Columbia was still a Crown colony (Duff 1964). In addition, the westernmost corner of Treaty 8 in the northeastern part of the province exists as the continuation of an Alberta treaty signed during the 1870s and concluded in the Athabasca District. Treaty 8 was signed during the original federal treaty process at approximately the time that Alberta entered Confederation

(Frideres and Gadacz 2005: 189; Brody 1981). However, most of the First Nations within what became British Columbia are without treaties and are currently seeking to realize their constitutional Aboriginal rights through the attainment of a treaty that would provide them with a land base, a formal national territory, sovereignty and the right to self-government (Tennant 1990). The fact that much of the First Nations' territory throughout the province is currently under claim, and also slated for industrial development

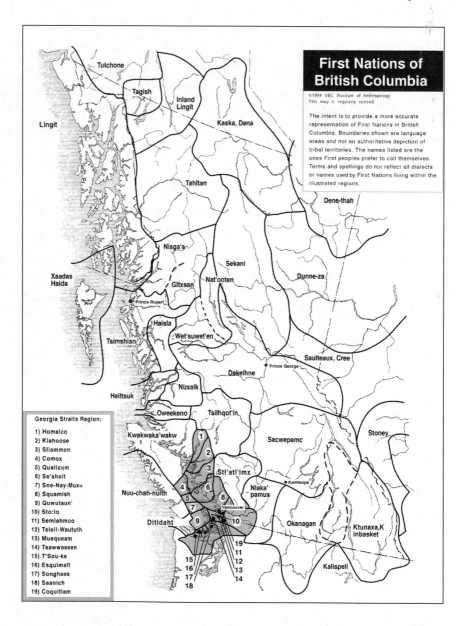

such as mining, logging and power projects, poses a significant threat for the potential of land surrenders for the many First Nations groups residing within the province.

The political history of First Nations in British Columbia has been characterized by an ongoing struggle to get their Aboriginal rights to the land, a distinct identity and self-government and self-determination formally recognized within a province that has refused to acknowledge land rights from its inception. In fact, the provincial government argued erroneously for more than a century that the Aboriginal land question within B.C. was settled when the Federal/Provincial Reserve Commission allocated reserves throughout the province in the 1860s. At that time, the Reserve Commission allocated parcels of residential land to the bands of approximately one to ten acres per family head, based on male heads of families (Duff 1965b; Frideres and Gadacz 2005: 189). The reserves were established on the basis of a subsistence agrarian model (foreign to the habits of the Aboriginals) and did not meet the requirements of their traditional hunting and gathering lifestyle. In fact, the allocated reserve lands have never met the livelihood needs of the many First Nations within British Columbia. Since the reserves were assigned, First Nations have experienced much higher increases in population in comparison to other groups in Canada. The government originally allocated the reserves with the thought that First Nations across Canada would quickly become assimilated into the dominant "whitestream" (Denis) majority, which was quickly growing in population size at that time (Frideres and Gadacz 2005: 65). However, contrary to the government of Canada's expectations, the First Nations populations throughout the country have largely held onto their special status, remained on reserves, retained their separateness and also proven to be the fastest growing population in Canada. Simultaneously, however, the area of Indian reserves — within British Columbia, in particular — has been shrinking, causing widespread hardship, the absence of a land base and generalized poverty and loss.

Thus, the problems of colonization, identity loss (in some regions) and the lack of land are likely to have been felt more profoundly in British Columbia over the past century, compared to the rest of Canada. In spite of the continuing problem, the constitutional process emerging within the courts with respect to overdue land settlements among First Nations within British Columbia does not reflect a true experiential, land-based, community-based Aboriginality. The process of Aboriginal identity formation in Canada resembles more closely that of a "state process" than one defined by First Nations community practices. As a result of a legacy of Aboriginal rights litigation at the level of the Supreme Court of Canada, First Nations peoples within British Columbia generally find it necessary to defend their Aboriginal rights in court and are, therefore, incurring a further risk of assimilation, rather than achieving a genuine land-based or community-based identity.

When Aboriginal land and right claims in British Columbia are being heard by the courts, First Nations are obliged to defend these claims against stiff opposition from the Crown, which seeks to refute their rights to land on the argument that they are invalid, possibly extinguished, or that occupancy never actually existed. Such a pattern has become established in large part because section 35 of the *Constitution Act* was originally left vague in its definitions of "Aboriginal rights," even though it argued that, "the rights obtained through the settlement of modern land claims would be considered constitutionally equivalent to treaty rights and hence would find constitutional protection under the Constitution Act, 1982" (Asch 1993: 37). Section 35, furthermore, states that "the existing Aboriginal and treaty rights of the Aboriginal peoples of Canada are hereby recognized and affirmed." It has been left to the courts to decide exactly what these rights are.

It can be argued that section 35 has been somewhat successful in establishing a new framework for addressing outstanding Aboriginal claims since it acknowledges Aboriginal people's occupation of the land since time immemorial. This concession within the Constitution has given rise to the existence of "Aboriginal rights" whenever such rights have not already been established by treaty. However, this same document has transferred the title and rights battle squarely into the domain of the courts and away from politics.

By the 1970s, Canadian courts had begun to acknowledge that Aboriginal peoples' occupation of the land from time immemorial gave rise to legal rights not provided for by treaty or statute. The constitutionalization of Aboriginal and treaty rights in 1982 established a new legal framework within which longstanding Aboriginal claims might be addressed. Section 35 of the *Constitution Act*, 1982 did not create rights; the provision recognizes and affirms the "existing Aboriginal and treaty rights" of the Aboriginal peoples of Canada and situates those rights outside the Canadian Charter of Rights and Freedoms with its section 1 limitation clause. The absence of terms defining the rights placed the task of interpreting the scope of section 35 squarely in the judicial sphere.

As a result of Supreme Court precedents from several landmark cases, especially *Nisga'a*, *Sparrow* and *Delgamuukw*, in pursuit of constitutional definitions, the identity markers of Aboriginality have been on a moving target, both provincially and federally, leading to a new cycle of cultural homogenization. This shift has been especially pronounced in the wake of the relatively recent Supreme Court of Canada judgment in *Gitxan-Wet'suwet'en versus the Crown* (*Delgamuukw*). While the effects of the *Gitxan-Wet'suwet'en* court cases were already beginning to percolate in the early 1990s, as First Nations leaders anticipated legal changes many First Nations throughout the province of

British Columbia quickly started to organize in order to "make *Delgamuukw* come alive" (Delgamuukw/Gisday'wa National Process).

Although *Delgamuukw* served as an incentive, the fact that the criteria for title and rights cases have largely been established at the discretion of the Crown means that the Aboriginal people perceive the positioning of the Canadian courts with respect to land claims to be unilateral, colonial and unfair. The criteria of the Canadian system of justice neither correspond with the priorities of a community-based Aboriginal worldview, nor accept that First Peoples lived in organized societies prior to contact as the first owners and inhabitants of the land. Nevertheless, the court's criteria of Aboriginal legitimacy are without exception rigidly followed, although they have merely been adapted from legal precedent and existing criteria, as drawn from various historical Aboriginal cases, such as, for example, the *Baker Lake* and *Sparrow*[3] cases. These criteria have never been subject to a comprehensive process of radical, crosscultural critique. In the legal process of rights determination, the Aboriginal people involved in land claims cases feel these criteria are unilaterally imposed by the federal government, which "requires both a detailed agenda that negotiations will follow and a statement limiting the issues to be negotiated" (Frideres and Gadacz 2005: 235), This streamlines and limits

the scope of the negotiations while further imposing a set of values on the process. As the Canadian court unilaterally lays out the criteria for rights determination, the founding values of such criteria do not properly reflect living community knowledge, embodied realities, Aboriginal customs or oral record. "Aboriginal people argue that their rights regarding the issues identified by the federal government are exchanged for legislated benefits" (235). Instead of facilitating the establishment of legal spaces in which Aboriginal identities could be negotiated and constructed by First Nations themselves, the law has arrogated to itself the power of naming Aboriginal identity and in so doing, has profoundly affected the processes by which individual and collective Aboriginal identities are constructed and maintained (Macklem 1993: 11, 12).

The Myth of Inadequate Civility

According to Macklem (1993), Crown sovereignty was legislated to supersede Aboriginal sovereignty during the period of colonial expansion. The legislation was justified on the basis of a perceived lack of civility on the part of the land's Native inhabitants. The inadequate civility (*terra nullius*, or vacant land)[4] argument provided a formal rationale upon which the territories of First Nations were deemed officially unoccupied and, therefore, available for settlement. Today, this same rationale of colonial extinguishment remains tacitly inherent in readings of the 1982 *Constitution Act*. Such colonial interpretive frameworks remain as points of inherent ethnocentrism at the root of current court processes. The doctrinal view of *"terra nullius,"* which in Canada, as in Australia, underpinned the new country's original view of Aboriginal people (and as found within the BNA *Act*) has been retained as a bias of the Crown in the resolution of Native claims, as it requires First Nations to provide proof of having been an organized society within their own territory at the time of contact. As a result of this implicit, underlying view, the 1982 Constitution's section 35 on Aboriginal rights portrays a pre-contact countryside so devoid of cultivation or development that sovereignty (or organized occupancy) was virtually impossible and thus must be proved prior to the granting of a land claim.

Their lands have been depicted as empty — *terra nullius* — a wilderness to be settled and turned to more productive pursuits by the presumed superior civilization of the new arrivals. In the same way, First Nations people were depicted as savage and untutored, wretched creatures in need of the civilizing influences of the settlers from Europe. This unflattering, self-serving and ultimately racist view coincided with the desire of British and colonial officials to acquire "Indian" lands for settlement with the minimum of legal or diplomatic formalities. This view prevailed throughout the nineteenth century, when the foundations for the *Indian Act* were being laid (Report of the Royal Commission on Aboriginal People, Vol. 1, Part II, Chapter 9). The inadequate civility principle underlies the federal *Indian Act*, which clearly exists as a living manifestation of these early views. Originally passed in 1876, under Parliament's constitutional responsibility for Indians and Indian lands, the Act has gone through the years in more or less its original form.

As a result of the pervading historical discourses on Aboriginal identity and rights which surround constitutional processes in Canada, the Crown has attempted to espouse that Aboriginal rights were duly extinguished with the entry of the provinces to Canada and thus must be rigorously corroborated if they are to be taken seriously (McEachern Decision 1991; Sterrit 1998: 8). It is this underlying perspective which sets the tone against which Aboriginal rights are currently being contested. The impact of *terra nullius* has been clearly addressed in the federal government's Report of the Royal Commission on Aboriginal Peoples, and thus it is no secret that the concept has been generally applied.

Delgamuukw

Since the *Delgamuukw* decision of 1997, as First Nations throughout British Columbia are seeking to prove and claim their Aboriginal rights, the "title and rights" battle has become more litigious and evidence driven, and less political in nature. On December 11, 1997, the Supreme Court of Canada released its decision on the Gitxan/Wet'suwet'en land claims case (known as

Delgamuukw), which marks the first time the Supreme Court has ruled defini-tively on the issue of Aboriginal title in Canada. The current bias in favour of court procedures and hearings, which followed as a result of *Delgamuukw*, has provided the state with a universal arbiter (the Supreme Court) through which it can negotiate, limit and profess what passes as the valid identifiers of Aboriginality and Aboriginal rights, thereby limiting the scope of what a First Nation is successfully able to argue. Thus, a culture of litigious practices and formalities circumscribes what passes as Aboriginal rights in Canada and, therefore, has been having a considerable impact on the formation of Native identity in recent years. However, the emergence of such a groomed litigious process of Aboriginal rights determination, pursuant to *Delgamuukw*, actually flies in the face of initiatives to de-colonize the Aboriginal peoples of Canada. Although, at the level of appearances, the federal and provincial governments advocate the advancement of Aboriginal rights, their actual processes may ultimately be spurious, entrenching colonial and mainstream values instead of First Nations' ones. In other words, litigious criteria with respect to Aboriginal rights serve on the one hand to perpetuate a generic Aboriginal identity, as was originally fostered in early government policies under colonialism and the *Indian Act*, and on the other, furthers earlier at-tempts to assimilate First Nations to the mainstream.

Prior to the flurry of litigious activity since *Delgamuukw* to defend Aboriginal rights, First Nations frequently resorted to community activism in order to have their rights recognized. Political activism, media campaigns, protests, political lobbies and so on generally offer unlimited scope for com-munity involvement and also for the free expression of Aboriginal identity, voice and claims. A shift towards an almost exclusive commitment to litigious processes in the resolution of First Nations' claims shows a growing bias in favour of colonial agendas, modernist discourse and Eurocentric thinking on the deposition of lands and rights determination. Such an ethnocentric process is merely a perpetuation of "internal colonialism" — colonialism perpetuated within a nation state, of which those affected are citizens.

However, current statist agendas with respect to land settlements and Aboriginal rights claims seem anathema to *Delgamuukw*'s original relaxation on formal evidence, which now encompasses oral testimonies, such as, elder accounts and stories, that the landmark ruling is famous for. "That is, they must accommodate the oral histories of Aboriginal societies, which may provide the only record of their past, and place such histories on an equal footing with documentary historical evidence" (Hurley 1999). However, court cases seem to focus largely on written and numeric evidence, expert testimonies and "white man's" maps (Behr 2009; Hudson 2009).

Moreover, although the *Delgamuukw* ruling made proving their land claim easier for the Gitxan claimants, who no longer had to prove occupancy since the time of European contact, the fact that court precedents in Canada require proof of continuous occupancy of the territories since the time of Crown sovereignty (Gitskan Chief's Office 2010) is re-shaping the political landscape for First Nations, bringing with it grave consequences. Such a process moves First Nations people closer to a rationalist Euro-colonial "ideal type" of land ownership and identity, where occupancy and Aboriginality are now subject to a highly litigious, statistical and factually groomed scientific process of occupational evidence, rather than being based on First Nations will, community experience and real human needs (Elsey 2001: 21, 22; Elsey 2009; Hudson 2009; Behr 2009).

The 1997 *Delgamuukw* ruling dictated that Aboriginal rights to land came second only to environmental conservation, which necessitated that a comprehensive process of consultation with the First Nation must take place by any government agency or stakeholder who seeks to infringe in any way on the First Nation's traditional territory. Thus, the *Gitxan/Wet'suwet'en* ruling provides a test case, offering what might be considered a *de facto* title to First Nations people throughout Canada, which allows First Nations the opportunity to legally defend their tribal territories and their titles in the face of any form of external intrusion, second only to concerns of environmental conservation, as long as continuous occupancy can be demonstrated. Thus, *Delgamuukw* is seen by most as a giant step forward in the advancement of Aboriginal rights. Having defined criteria for proving Aboriginal title (relatively exclusive occupation prior to Crown sovereignty that has been relatively continuous to the present), the Court outlined a justification test for infringements of Aboriginal title based on general principles established in its previous section 35 decisions (Hurley 1999). Thus, the range of legislative objectives capable of justifying infringements of Aboriginal title is broad, while the nature of the government's fiduciary duty is determined by the nature of title. The fact that Aboriginal title encompasses the right to exclusive use and occupation of the land is relevant to the degree of scrutiny of the infringing measure or action; the fact that it also encompasses the right to choose how the land is used influences the nature and scope of the Crown's obligation to consult the Aboriginal group whose title is infringed, and the fact that title has an economic component affects the amount of compensation due.

However, the most recent identifier of Aboriginal rights (*Delgamuukw*) also transfers First Nations more firmly into the arena of court hearings, and it has yet to be seen whether the priority it awards to Aboriginal evidence — oral evidence, over written — will unambiguously be upheld. In the paper "*Delgamuukw*: A Legal Straight Jacket for Oral Histories," Napoleon talks of the original frustration of the Gitxan/Wet'suwet'en in having their oral testimonies on their spiritual relationship to the land validated and upheld at the level of the Supreme Court. Although judge McEachern's ruling was overturned by the Supreme Court of Canada, the flagrant ethnocentrism present in McEachern's hearings shows the entrenchment and complexity of existing problems associated with court-based misinterpretation, value judgements and crosscultural misreadings. The courts have failed to successfully problematize the crosscultural misrepresentations that have historically been present, and are still present, in the long Canadian history of Aboriginal claims. In a word, the courts are "ethnocentric" and largely lacking in the criteria necessary to insure an unbiased, de-colonized, crosscultural approach. The literature necessary for genuine crosscultural dialogue, for the most part, remains unwritten, and the academic debates from First Nations intellectuals, although crucially necessary, are in many cases still unpublished.

This chapter problematizes how Chief Justice McEachern of the British Columbia Supreme Court responded when a Gitxan witness, Gwaans, presented her *adaawk*[5] as evidence of Gitxan land ownership and social organization. The court was not able to hear or accept the *adaawk* as presented — as a legal and political institution rather than a simple cultural artefact or chronological history record. The forms of expression, symbolism and interconnections between the worlds of spirits, humans and animals proved to be beyond the grasp of the trial judge. Will the *adaawk* be treated any differently in future litigation? This chapter problematizes a number of concerns, such as the judiciary applying a reductionist approach to the *adaawk*, and evaluating the *adaawk* according to the rules of court instead of those inherent in the *adaawk* (Napoleon 2005: 123–55).

Although it is through an accurate understanding of Aboriginal worldviews and embodied community concerns that de-colonization in British Columbia and Canada will start to become a reality, new paradigms for Aboriginal evidence have yet to be developed, and instead more scientific, electronic and technological forms of evidence are being required. "Stan Persky, the author of *Delgamuukw*, points out in his commentary that not only did the court impart that Aboriginal stories matter, but the Aboriginal title is recognized in both common and constitutional law and it does have specific content and implications" (Napoleon 2005).

As far as the First Nations' title and rights struggle is concerned, Native people themselves are currently involved in a foot race to preserve their cultural knowledge and terrestrial identity before time, industrial development and the litigious apparatuses of the modernist state erase their historical threads to an immediate and practising past. It would seem, judging from the number of title and rights cases now before the courts, that it is both an imposed and desperate race, which seeks to routinize and rationalize First Nations' claims in the interests of continuing globalization and industrial agendas of the multinationals. Not only is First Nations' potential for a land base at stake, but cultural and spiritual identity also hangs in the balance. The physical survival of Native bands is also at stake, in that they are expected to quickly gather enough "cultural identifiers" to give concrete, empirical and legal proof of their continuous and unbroken attachment to place.

For the First Nations of British Columbia, land shared between tribes has frequently been formalized by the sharing of meat or fish and acknowledged through the respect shown for the landmarks and customs of the other tribe. Thus, the land itself has served as a text that guides First Nations peoples' actions that were not formally legislated. Often such understandings about the other party's use patterns within a shared landscape are represented within a shared body of folklore, or spiritual or "poetic" representations of the land subscribed to by two or more tribal groups (Teit 1912b: 1909). Such ancestral Aboriginal practices are at odds with a Eurocentric commitment to hard evidence and utilitarian values, as presented in the new legislative and interpretive frameworks pursuant to section 35 of the Constitution. However, the courts see the world "from one perspective," which can generally be summed up as being colonial, rationalistic and ethnocentric (Denis 1997). The difficult problem of Aboriginal rights determination has been copiously defined by a series of legal precedents over the last thirty years through the modernist and litigious procedures of the Canadian justice system. Due to current interpretive frameworks, however, emerging from a long-standing legacy of court judgments, a heavy burden of empirical proof is now being placed upon all First Nations — especially in British Columbia — actively pursuing their rights to land. In order to receive constitutional recognition of their Aboriginal rights, the many treaty-less First Nations of British Columbia are currently being mandated to corroborate legal claims of a relative exclusivity of property ownership over their own ancestral territories, based on continuous pre-contact occupancy, which must be proven through empirical written evidence and mapped out with the use of cartographical procedures, or what could otherwise be referred to as "white man's maps" (Brody 1981).

Assimilation and the Land Question

In today's neoliberal, utilitarian climate in British Columbia, the question of First Nations' rights are being subjected more than ever before to a pervasive commitment to privatization and commodification of lands and resources. However, a less obvious and more insidious pattern has been brewing over the past ten years, due to a preponderance of new administrative and litigious reasoning emerging at the level of the Supreme Court of Canada. Today, comprehensive land claims and treaty projects abound in First Nations communities throughout British Columbia. The many projects still in existence encompass legal research, policy analysis and education in the interests of effective implementation of the opportunities inherent in the new judgment. Currently, as a result, the First Nations pursuing their rights and title are expected to prove these to the satisfaction of the courts with respect to section 35. *Delgamuukw* thus has provided a "test outline" in Canada for proving "Aboriginal title." The process of rights determination has been considerably confounded, even though it seems to have been moved forward. Asch's words, at this juncture, are historically telling: "The governments of Canada have remained faithful to the proposition that Canadian state sovereignty 'extinguished' Aboriginal sovereignty as an orienting principle in negotiations with Aboriginal nations concerning Aboriginal self-government" (1993: 43). Thus, in the absence of formal sovereignty validations for First Nations people, it has become commonplace for the Crown to negotiate legalistic and economic interpretations of land claims as the leading "identity marker" in First Nations' title and rights battles.

It is particularly insidious that the current discursive dominance of formal, litigious processes is creating a generic and disembodied vision of Aboriginal identity that favours utilitarian values of claims, while overlooking questions of First Nations' poetics, collectivism, self-determination and will. As a result of these juridical markers, a so-called legal Aboriginal identity has been emerging that in turn risks re-shaping both the collective and individual identities of the First Nations people. Aboriginal self-understanding, in this event, would follow a process of reflexivity upon the continuum of definitive litigious processes. Although intercultural translation always involves distortion, some forms of translation are grosser than others. Several Occidental readings, or re-descriptions, of First Nations' cultures are always possible and the nature of such readings depend on the goals and intentions with which each reader approaches the Aboriginal subject. As Turpel points out (1990), courts fail to take cultural differences seriously. Thus, juridical readings are one type of reading that typically involves a gross sense of distortion and, therefore, injury to Aboriginal ways (Denis 1997). Cultural differences between Aboriginal peoples and the Canadian state and its legal system represent problems of conceptual reference for which there is no common grounding or authoritative foothold. Necessarily, we can't "decide" the substance of cultural differences from a position of a particular institutional and conceptual cultural framework; each culture is capable of sensitivity to the basic condition of difference and should develop crosscultural relations accordingly (Turpel 1990: 14).

The decisions since *Delgamuukw* that require legal proofs of occupancy in aid of Aboriginal title fast track an insidious and often unrecognized assimilation. Such a generic identity formula tends to render First Nations people invisible in terms of who they truly are. Macklem states: "Legal Aboriginal identity in turn has shaped the individual and collective identities of Aboriginal people. Individual and collective Aboriginal self-understandings have been shaped and constituted in part by a complex form of resistance and acceptance of aspects of an Aboriginal identity that the law holds out to First Nations as their own" (1993: 12). And Denis points out: "Suffice it to say, second, that the call to silence does not serve First Nations because of the inescapable reality that, in Canada as elsewhere, they must live surrounded by a majority of whites" (1997: 46). As explained above, legal proof of Aboriginal rights tends to focus on ancestral pre-contact occupancy, exclusivity of ownership and continuous Aboriginal territorial use-patterns. Such identifiers revolve around the hub of colonial conceptions of property ownership but do little to move forward the agenda of First Nations' inherent political will and self-determination. Rather, they tend to freeze political will in the direction of an administrative agenda that addresses the so-called constitutional process as opposed to the expression and advancement of a self-willing, self-selecting, community-based Aboriginal identity.

In response to the pervading litigious climate, a plethora of professional agendas have emerged that steer attention away from the immediate expression of real-life, embodied concerns of the various communities and people. For example, within land claims trials, "First Nations have been obliged to engage professional expert witnesses to prove their pre-sovereign occupancy of a given package of land" (Hudson 2009). The necessity of experts seems to suggest the need for a higher order of expert proof alongside the already acknowledged "oral proof" for which *Delgamuukw* has been celebrated. The "oral proofs," by way of elders' testimonies and local, anecdotal accounts, open up the chance for experientially driven statements and embodied forms of identity claims that speak to community sentiments and embodied truths, which are aired in the legal process and can be heard from the stand. However, expert witnessing that puts professionals and factual accounts in control of the evidential processes diverts attention away from Aboriginality, to a more carefully groomed, litigiously driven administrative agenda. In most cases, this agenda favours "white man's maps," economic models and utilitarian (economic) interpretations of Aboriginal issues (Behr 2009; Brody 1981; Brealy 1995). In addition, the interpretive frameworks of section 35, which outline the passing of a "legal test" of continuous "pre-sovereign occupancy," steer the legitimization of "native title" towards models of European-style property ownership and in the direction of colonial expectations.

The White Man's Maps

Litigious trends that favour rationalist or "atomistic" paradigms, which stress exclusive ownership, can be observed at work in emerging cases of joint use of territorial regions by different tribes (for hunting, for example). Here, there has been an imposed requirement to prove exclusive occupancy of a specific First Nation over a claimed terrestrial package (DGNP). Even the B.C. treaty process itself maps out this exclusivity of ownership. The litigious pattern pursuant to section 35, requiring proof of stable and continuous occupancy, is not representative of the experiential web of First Nations' use. Territorial occupancy and use, rather, have been highly elastic and flexible while generally based on seasonal and cyclical harvesting patterns at different, far-flung locations amid networks of shared, territorial reciprocation between tribes within a nexus of inter-tribal kinship connections (Teit in McMillan 1988: 155). For example, Bouchard and Kennedy (1998) show that many people from diverse tribes congregated at fishing spots, such as Six Mile at the confluence of the Bridge and Fraser Rivers, in the plateau region during fishing season. They, furthermore, show that visitors who engaged in resource sharing with the Fraser River Lillooet had the rights of full participation within this public fishery.

We have no way of knowing how many Indians from outside of Stl'atl'imx territory were among those met by Simon Fraser. But Sam Mitchell maintained that in former times, Shuswap people from as far away as Kamloops, as well as Okanagan people from Vernon, visited the fisheries in the vicinity of Six Mile and participated in the fishing there. And on several occasions Sam Mitchell mentioned that anyone could fish at Six Mile. In a 1928 summary report on the Bridge River/Six Mile fisheries, federal fisheries guardian B. Cherry wrote that the Indians fishing there were from Lillooet, Bridge River, Fountain, Cayoosh Creek, D'Arcy, Shalalth, Pavilion, 22 Mile and Hat Creek (in Bouchard and Kennedy 1998: 314).

The attempt of locating Native claims within Western paradigms of ownership and access is convincingly falsified by the evidence of shared resource sites, flexible and elastic political structuring and cyclic and transitory sites of habitation. In the plateau culture region, for example, during the era of early contact, the lack of leadership positions (above the level of winter village) meant that people likely didn't have a definite concept of themselves as being either Stl'atl'imx or Nlaka'pamux. The methods of negotiating and agreeing upon differing levels of terrestrial access between groups have tended to be informal, highly familial, reciprocal and cyclic in nature — as opposed to static and formal (Teit 1900; Hudson 1996). Nevertheless, such patterns are not reflected in the current constitutional process, which tends to perceive boundaries as firm and unbending. Such forms of validation shift Native identity markers once and for all in favour of European land ownership paradigms and in favour of rationalist values over experiential values that are embodied and felt. It can further be argued that the traditional use studies being undertaken in support of the B.C. treaty process, pursuant to section 35 and constitutional precedents, are an administrative process that serves to reveal Aboriginal presence in terms of "scientistic," measurable, graphable zones of purposeful activity, which can be devolved onto mutually exclusive economic units. Such routinizing templates must be problematized for their denial of both the experiential and affective affiliation to a landscape with which the First Nations are profoundly "self-identified." The attempt of locating Native claims within Western paradigms of ownership and access is convincingly falsified by the evidence of shared resource sites, flexible and elastic political structuring and cyclic and transitory sites of habitation.

The insistence on rationalistic, litigious processes over all other social and cultural forms of expression, identity and will is troubling. The fact that institutional utensils of the Occidental, modernist state have prevailed in Aboriginal rights and identity determination over experiential markers, as in folkloric accounts, community letters, elders' testimonies, art works, political movements and so on, speaks to an ongoing silencing and "delegitimization" of Aboriginal culture and voice. Although *Delgamuukw* has provided a useful tool in pushing the resolution of land claims forward, it also perpetuates the rationalist, colonial and institutional agendas of the Canadian state's unilateral political processes. The litigious agenda discussed above runs the risk of further silencing, invisibilizing and "delegitimizing" First Nations of British Columbia, who possess cultural legacies founded upon oral tradition and are embedded in traditional forms of knowledge. All of these First Nations have valued ancestral identities that interface with a spiritual, poetic/folkloric and experiential meaning of land, and that stand in contrast to European "Enlightenment" identity principles (Elsey 2001). Native meanings of most things are different to those of the European; thus, First Nations have existed since contact under what can be termed a "Euro-colonial grid of meaning" that renders First Nations culture invisible to the European eye (Elsey 2001; Brody 1981). This tendency is nowhere better demonstrated than by the use of the "white man's maps" in demonstrating the dimensions of an Aboriginal land base. As Denis states: "Re-described through 'Western' eyes, Aboriginal ways will be necessarily distorted; there is no escaping this" (1997: 45). Since *Delgamuukw*, Aboriginal identity markers seem to be shifting in order to better accommodate a European/colonial ideal-type of utilitarian meanings, scientistic process and private-ownership.

> Some would conclude that people not possessed of an Aboriginal point-of-view have no option but to remain silent, that any attempt to account for Aboriginal ways in occidental terms is cultural appropriation, doing violence to Aboriginal people. (Denis 1997: 45)

The Poetics of Place

In contrast to litigious definitions and "white man's maps," Aboriginal identity markers have historically been drawn from the holistic, spiritual view of the land of First Nations people as captured by the following ethnographic example. In the case of the Gitxan, the traditional identity markers of Aboriginality were rooted in the meaning of the land, as given in a spiritual iconography of place, for example the *adaawk* (mentioned above), as a relationship between the people, the Creator and the territory that goes back to the last ice age, which was cited in the 1992 court hearing of the Gitxan/Wet'suwet'en claim by then chief of the Canadian Ethnology Service, Andrea Laforet.

> *Adaawk*; she looks at *adaawk* and see the authority in it. The authority, says Andrea, derived originally from encounters between human ancestors and animal, encounter between supernatural beings; told exclusively by the chief or the chief's designate as a prerogative and function of the chief's office, in the feast hall. *Adaawk*; she looks at continuity and observes that passed from generation to generation to one designated chief to the other. *Adaawk* has steps; time unsegmented. Lineage histories began following the early flood, which caused the dispersion and migration to their own territories. Interdependence, each *adaawk* is expected to have integrity in and of itself. The principle narrative is supported by crests, names, songs, totem poles, and other lineage properties. (Laforet (1992) in Ken Harris 1999)

Gitxan iconography of place (alluded to above) spoke to the terrestrial experiences of an ancestral house group, or what are known to the Gitxan as Wilps (Cove 1982: 8). In this example, which serves as a relatively characteristic explanation of hereditary coastal identity, a matrilineal house group is merged with their surrounding territory in experiential and folkloric terms. Typical of other First Nations within British Columbia, who have traditionally been hunter-gatherers, their traditional territories revolve around a salmon fishing river and its watershed's boundaries. The watershed boundaries also mark the borders of a dialectical, or linguistic, group. Therefore, the claim to nationhood follows the claim to cultural, spiritual, linguistic and terrestrial identity among like speakers, thus proving the relationship between cultural identity and terrestrial homelands. Use of the territory, the ancestral experience out on the land and the spiritual encounters of the ancestors with various spirit powers are all expressed in the iconography of the house or territory, which represents the symbolism and meaning of everything that inheres in the idea of being a Gitxan (Elsey 2001; Cove 1982).

"A House was deemed to have title to a territory because it had merged its essence with a piece of land" (Cove 1987a). That essence was its stock of supernatural powers, acquired by ancestors of the house from spirits (*naxnox*) who had taken on physical forms to live in the same domain as humans (Cove 1982).

For the many Aboriginal tribes in British Columbia, the interpreting and articulating of landscape is a primary concern within the oral tradition of the people (Cove 1982; Thornton 1997; Duff 1959; deLeguna 1972). Characteristically, legends as well as "symbolic wealth" — a family's stock of crests, dances, songs and masks, for example — are contextualized geographically with respect to a tribal territory's corresponding ancestral locations. These locations frequently serve to demonstrate the age-old self-identification of a given tribal people with their respective landscape. In many cases, it is the stock of symbolic wealth that tends to contextualize this tribal people's belonging and spirituality as being-on-the-land (Elsey 2001). The terrestrial identity of First Nations people has largely been one of imbrication (or connectedness and involvement) with the land as a surrounding territory, or as a homeland, which is a part of the people themselves.

Such a holistic interpretation of Aboriginality was present to a greater extent in the battle for title and rights in British Columbia during the political ferment of the 1980s, when the Aboriginal rights climate was intensely more political than it was litigious. At that time, First Nations people in great numbers sang ancestral songs, danced clan dances and spoke out in the media and on stages around the province in the interest of First Nations' land preservation and rights. A holistic and experiential notion of Aboriginal identity politically, aesthetically and terrestrially loomed large. First Nations political leaders began collaborating with leading environmental groups in the interests of land preservation; the importance of the land as having both an aesthetic and experiential value was prominent. For example, while fighting for Stein Valley preservation, former Nlaka'pamux chief, Ruby Dunstan, made constant metaphoric associations during her innumerable speeches between the land and Native spirituality as the people's deepest sense of their experience and survival as First Nations. The following words by Chief Dunstan give voice to this point:

> They started talking about going into log. By this time the elders were calling me and saying, "you can't let them go in there and log, because that's our fridge, that's our pantry. If you let them go in there our people are going to die ... not only because of the food, but because of the spiritual things that are in that valley." (in Neel 1992: 47)

Throughout the 1980s, mainstream environmental organizations, such as the Western Wilderness Committee, and First Nations wilderness preservation groups and the ten-member Wilderness Advisory Committee and the Save the Stein Coalition, began to advance complementary dual agendas of ecological conservation and Aboriginal land rights (M'Gonigle and Wickwire 1988; Suzuki 2006). In most cases, the dual position revolved around the meaning of the land as an "experiential value," as opposed to an economic or utilitarian value. Much of this activity died down in the wake of the *Delgamuukw* decision, while the more litigious and factual evaluation of Aboriginal identity and rights, as discussed above, has widely taken place. Thus, a directional shift has occurred, away from experiential notions of identity in favour of formal, legal definitions and proofs that valorize the tenets of private property and non-Aboriginal forms of being on the land, thus minimizing the spiritual, aesthetic and political (experiential values) of Aboriginal identity and rights.

Conclusions

The 1997 Gitxan/Wet'suwet'en judgment shifted identity markers of Aboriginality largely into the domain of court proceedings and routinized legislative processes. In this domain, the Aboriginal rights of First Nations are either denied or affirmed on the basis of abstract, rationalist, constitutional definitions and evidential proofs. Such methods promote a generic "non-embodied" Aboriginal identity that does not speak squarely to the Aboriginal experience, the unique will of the specific First Nations tribes or to the political issues of self-determination and sovereignty, which get side-tracked in favour of colonialist concerns. The process has marked a qualitative shift away from the climate of political activism and free speech, observable in many First Nations communities before 1992. As a result of the more litigious agendas, it seems likely that the genuine First Nations voice could be both silenced and diminished simultaneously, with the mandate to respond to the legislative opportunity provided by the *Delgamuukw* carrot. Thus, the fear is that identity markers of Aboriginality have been shifting to favour legislative agendas over living community concerns.

Litigious views, as encouraged by the courts, likely fast track assimilation of First Nations at the expense of a genuine place-based Aboriginal identity. By alternative, a regionally based poetics would speak to the unique oral and aesthetic representations, ancestral storyscapes and a shared life on the territory. In the litigious domain, evidential proofs of claims with respect to the Aboriginal rights are either denied or affirmed on the basis of constitutional definitions, which are abstract, rationalist and Eurocentric utilitarian. This book demonstrates that the First Nations' day-to-day reality of "being on the land" harkens back to the existence of a territorial poetics, which differs for every First Nation, but which rests on each group's oral traditions and ancestral folkloric, linguistic representations.

A study of the diverse folkloric traditions of the First Nations within British Columbia clearly shows the existence of a terrestrial poetics and the spirituality of the territory, as well as a distinct self-identification of people with both the animate and inanimate features of their surrounding landscape. Such an orientation speaks to an identity of enfoldment between the people and their territory, which renders them inseparable from the territory and landforms that for centuries have surrounded them. Thus, treaties and claims that focus on cash settlements and other economic devices in the establishment of monetary worth or "white man's maps" do little to advance de-colonization. Utilitarian, economic models of land do not help to solve the conundrum of a de-colonizing First Nations' identity within British Columbia. The existence value, the spiritual value and the folkloric value of the territory loom large for the many First Nations people within B.C. who still live close to the land.

Terrestrial identity through imbrication can be contrasted to an identity and self-worth that is derived through ownership, as is a common thread within almost all Eurocentric models of identity and selfhood (Elsey 2001). Such a complete self-identification with the territory, which renders the First Nations inhabitants virtually inseparable from it, results from an age-old familiarity and closeness with the land, which is embedded within a collective worldview and is passed down as a body of orally transmitted stories. Throughout the region now known as British Columbia, each Aboriginal group within a tribal territory possessed its own unique folkloric and oral traditions, which were owned and passed down within families. The many stories and traditions (such as hereditary masks, poles, frontlets, dances and songs) are connected to the storied and named places on the hunting territory, which in many cases people visit, identify with strongly and also love (Cruikshank 1990; Cove 1987a; Brody 1981).

In sum, the Aboriginal identity of those who are members of First Nations territories is the direct result of the hereditary and ancestral interaction that has occurred within an ecological region over centuries of terrestrial occupation and harvesting. The self-identification that has occurred over centuries between the Natives and the land within British Columbia has been passed down through the oral traditions since "time out of mind." Such a legacy provides a connectedness with the land which is both divorced from and at odds with the detached Cartesian based worldview of the European mainstream consciousness that has characterized the majority thinking of B.C.'s population since Confederation and the modernist state, which has seen Aboriginal claims largely in economic as opposed to cultural and spiritual terms. The identity, spirituality and worldview of the diverse First Nations inhabitants throughout the province have in reality been fostered through an intimate, daily relationship with the territory. These are territories that are not formally owned but are largely shared amongst a wide spectrum of related people, family groupings and kin, who are likely to exhibit land rights and group membership across a number of different tribes. The existence of a First Nations iconography and poetics of the territory generally spells out these terrestrial relations through stories and land marks which bear a telling, often of how certain parts of the land should be used and of all that has gone on there. The self-identification that has occurred over centuries between the First Nations and the land give testimony to a holistic terrestrial consciousness which is dissimilar and unrelated to the Cartesian based worldview of the European mainstream. The European view sees individuals as separate and detached, while it perceives the land to be alienable, material, private property. Thus, the Western view of land is anathema to the First Nations' view, which is holistic and inseparable from the identity of the people themselves.

Notes

1. Aboriginal author and scholar Jeanette Armstrong in "Sharing One's Skin" explains the deep ancestral connection between her Okanagan people and the land, as if the land were a part of their skin.
2. Treaties signed at the time of Canada's Confederation are considered inadequate and are up for renegotiation mainly because they do not give the First Nations, who possess them, rights to prevent development on their territory or rights to resources, such as minerals, as a treaty right.
3. *Baker Lake* and *Sparrow* are two Aboriginal rights cases that have had an influence on Aboriginal constitutional law in Canada. *Baker Lake* was an Inuit based case; *Sparrow* was a Supreme Court case involving a Stó:lō fisherman in the Fraser River.
4. In Canada, the *BNA Act* of 1867 did not include support for Aboriginal rights and instead embraced terra nullius, or the notion that upon the arrival of Europeans Canadian land was devoid of civilized life and thus open for unencumbered settlement and nationhood.
5. The *adaawk* is the Gitxan oral history or knowledge that represents the relationship between the people, the Creator and the territory, and which is believed to go back to the last ice-age. The *adaawk* of each lineage affirms Gitxan cultural identity and care of the land and is maintained through theatre, songs and dances from the Gitxan heritage.

Chapter 3

The Poetics of Self and Land

> If you were to apply the notion of social contract to a Native concept of land ownership what you will find is that Native people are only one party to the contract. These trees, those rocks, the deer, that fish swimming around, they're all parties to the contract. And that's why Native people say we could never sell, we could never surrender the land, because it doesn't belong to us. If you're going to have a sale, you're going to have to go ask the deer, you know, consult the rocks, see if its ok with them, see, cause we're only one party to the contract. (Leroy Littlebear, of the Blackfoot people, at the Stein Voices for the Wilderness festival, August 1987, in M'Gonigle and Wickwire 1988: 176)

As explained in the last chapter, the establishment of Native rights in Canada since Confederation has focused on: 1) proving that claimants occupied their territories during pre-sovereign times; and 2) determining that during pre-sovereign times they were part of a so-called organized society. Establishing such claims subjects First Nations to highly restrictive court procedures that define, circumscribe and limit Aboriginal rights and claims to that which can be legally proven within the context of modernist procedures of Canadian justice and on the basis of demonstrable empirical evidence.

Litigious approaches employed by the Crown rely on hard evidence in the realization of Native claims and expect that claims, without exception, should conform to bounded, evidential explanations of First Nations' lands and territories, for example, as found on "white man's" regional maps. Such an emphasis on empirical proof undermines the primacy of First Nations' oral accounts and storied explanations about land use and occupancy as told and used by the Native people themselves (Cruikshank 1990: 52–65). Oral testimonies and stories can provide us with a living map, similar to what can be offered by the process of "ground-truthing,"[1] where the actual physical travels of elders are penciled onto a regional map depicting where they went to harvest certain animals, where they went do fishing and hunting etc. (Brody 1981). Oral maps, or descriptive journeys through the territory for the purposes of getting food, are not flat, one-dimensional graphs depicting hard boundaries and divisions. By comparison they are sensuous, elastic, picturesque and free floating. Stories are often oral records of the territory; they depict what went on at certain important spots on the land in earlier times and record the history of the First Nation's people of a region, thereby encoding historical information into oral memory. Such maps and stories are living representations of what people actually did at a certain place, and they speak squarely to the question of "authentic dwelling,"[2] or what people did in the embodied sense within their territory.

The advancement of such a phenomenological, or "anti-rationalist," discourse, located within the Aboriginal setting, provides a cogent critique to utilitarian resource management's approaches to the environment and to the rationalist techniques of the Canadian justice system. In Western utilitarian models, economic value, in the broad sense, is considered relevant to all — it's viewed as a universal measurement of true value (Evernden 1985: 9). Thus, forests are seen as timber stands and rivers as power projects. The utilitarian, resource-management perspective makes a recorded inventory of terrestrial sites, evaluated on the basis of economic advantage and social benefits. British Columbia's Aboriginal peoples, in almost all cases, evaluate their terrestrial environments using a different scale, one that highlights the quintessential importance of the land's meaning within the Aboriginal notion of selfhood.

A painful reminder to us on the ills of prioritizing utilitarian values and ignoring First Nations autonomy and selfhood, is the outcome of the James Bay Cree Agreement in 1975. The James Bay Agreement was made by the federal government to facilitate the Le Grand River Hydro Project, thereby giving Hydro Quebec over three hundred kilometres of ancestral Cree hunting territories in northern Quebec in exchange for $225 million (Feit 1995: 209). The project has had disastrous social and cultural consequences for the Cree people, who were relocated from their tribal settlements and faced the flooding of their ancestral territories, which resulted in the widespread loss of their culture and their traditional hunting life. Matthew Coon-Come, Grand Chief of the Grand Council of the Crees of Quebec, the plaintiff in the James Bay Hydro Hearing held in Amsterdam during March of 1992, said:

> The Cree have been living in this area for 5000 years. We use the land for hunting, fishing, and trapping. Because of the building of dams the fish are polluted with mercury. The villages are changed socially — there is more drug and alcohol abuse. Our future is determined by outsiders. The impact of James Bay 1 is great: the fish are poisoned, water flows are reversed, there are climate changes and there are social problems. Our inheritance is under the water,

we are unsure about the future. Other people, outsiders, make decisions about our future. (Grand Council of the Crees <www.ca/
links/links.php #ener>)

In spite of, and perhaps because of, the ensuing problems of the Le Grand
project and relocations, "on February 7, 2002, the James Bay Cree went on
and signed a deal with the Quebec government that allows continued hydro
development in northern Quebec. The agreement gives the Cree $3.5 billion
over 50 years" (CBC Archives, Broadcast, February 7, 2002). This has to a
large degree ended of their arboreal, hunting existence.

After pondering the problems associated with the case of the James Bay
Cree, it seemed fitting to engage in a study on the meaning of land for First
Nations within British Columbia and to demonstrate the importance of the
territory from an environmental and ancestral standpoint, rather than from
an economic standpoint. Therefore, the objective of this study is to offer an
environmental discourse, arrived at through phenomenological concepts,
which demonstrates how the unique regional landscapes of the First Nations
of British Columbia exist as Native people's own self-identification, thus
having an existence akin to that of skin — as opposed to monetary or utilitarian advantage. The discourse of European phenomenology demonstrates
the existence of a set of dichotomous principles at the core of mainstream
European thought, such as subject versus object, mind versus body, bodily
inside versus outside, self versus other, and nature versus culture, as well
as human versus nonhuman. This dualistic thinking, which resulted from
Cartesian rationalism, has been formative in Western notions of the self. Such
a worldview places nature at a remove as an object, separate and detached
from humans. However, the First Nations folkloric depiction of self, as one
flowing together with the non-human world, offers a challenge — from both a
philosophical and environmental standpoint — to the modernist, mainstream
"whitestream"[3] perspectives.

The holistic perspective of self, body and world as interconnected looks
at the human body as an extended body, including all that it touches and
experiences. Thus the senses are the means by which humans relate to and
identify with their world. The territory becomes the existence of their hearing
and their ears (as the known territorial sounds around them), the sensuous
contours of the land and flora and fauna as their bodily feeling and touch
(it is their skin as associated with all they touch), their eyes as their seeing
(the landscape of their accustomed view). To summarize the traditional territory's meaning in utilitarian terms is to overlook its "real" meaning to the
Aboriginal people. In short, a utilitarian view, which is ultimately reductionist,
amputates the land from the people as though it were one of their limbs.
Such an approach amounts to taking away their skin, an expression I have

often heard within Aboriginal communities in the region. Elder Annie York's pictograph interpretation of a rock bolder in the Stein Valley is telling. The rock boulder and its painting represented an old lady who had power, who said, "My eyes will be far out to watch over you; she was watching over her grandchildren. Her eyes (her vision) were embodied in the rock" (York, Daly and Arnett 1993: 218).

Aboriginal being and place, therefore, are very different from the utilitarian-focused approaches employed in Aboriginal land claims and treaty processes in British Columbia. Contemporary traditional-use studies, which inform the treaty process, rely heavily on conventional utilitarian and ecological models, with their itemization of use-sites as mappable resources. The empirical approach is alive and well at all levels of Native claims settlement, whose processes view Aboriginal lands largely from the perspective of their monetary value and therefore usually seek to settle territorial claims through cash settlements (Duff 1964: 61).

The intention of this work is to illustrate, on the basis of the extant Aboriginal folklore, that the Aboriginal peoples of British Columbia view their world in a manner that contrasts sharply with economic models of environmental space. A survey of many written accounts of First Nations people in British Columbia, within the disciplines of anthropology and Native studies, has convinced me that First Nations are self-identified with and inseparable from their ancestral territories, which provide the very firmament of their meaning system and identity.

The analysis offered within this work rests on the application and development of three interrelated concepts in order to situate the discourse of phenomenology and environmental sociology within the Aboriginal setting. The concepts of "enfoldment," "storyscape" and *"poiesis,"* serve as a threefold structure within which to analyze the spatiality of human selfhood with regards to Aboriginal concerns. I analyze First Nations folklore within British Columbia on these three interconnected levels, moving from the most concrete, experiential level to the abstract, symbolic level, or that of the self's expression.

Enfoldment

Throughout the study, the concept of "enfoldment" is used to explain the importance of the unity of meaning and being within a territorial *"poiesis,"* or poetics. This concept problematizes and transcends Cartesian dualities of "subject versus object" and the hegemony of mathematical or empirical forms of knowing over Indigenous ways of knowing, meaning and being. As Indigenous ways of knowing are holistic and non-compartmentalized, "enfoldment" incorporates a phenomenological approach to being that speaks to transcendence of subject versus object and, therefore, to the interrelatedness of human and non-human beings within a shared life process and shared territory. In other words, the environmental discourses of Indigenous scholarship, sociological phenomenology, anthropological phenomenology and so on argue for a holistic or unbroken continuity between humans and non-human aspects of the world and the territory (as found in such authors as Evernden, Abram, Ingold, Feit, Scott, Basso, Cruikshank, Feld, Kahn et al., and also in Absolon 2011, Atleo 2004, Armstrong 2000, Couture 1991).

Thus, the term "enfoldment" helps us to conceptualize the unbroken or holistic experience of being between an Indigenous people and their ancestral territory. The holistic perspective can also be described as an "extended body experience" (Merleau-Ponty 1968) which incorporates the land and humans into one unbroken unity of meaning and being (Ingold 1996), as if into one skin, as expressed by Jeannette Armstrong in her 2006 article "Sharing One Skin":

> It is my body that is being torn, deforested and poisoned by "development." Every fish, plant, insect, bird and animal that disappears is part of me dying. I know all their names and I touch them with my spirit. (Armstrong 2006)

It is in the interests of conceptualizing this unity that we introduce the concept of "enfoldment." Thus, spirituality is shared with other non-human persons and geophysical bodies (Ingold 1996; Basso 1996; Charlie Mack in Kennedy and Bouchard, 2010) within a surrounding territory, or storyscape (Greider and Garkovich 1994). In many instances within this study, the territorial surroundings (both animal and geophysical) of the Aboriginal groups under discussion are ascribed with personhood and spirituality and thus exemplify enfoldment, as the human experience is interconnected with features of the landscape such that people are spiritually inseparable from it. This personalization of non-human agents inhering within the Aboriginal, territorial landscape can be seen, for instance, in examples of geological landmarks, such as unusually shaped stones or boulders, like the Transformer stones that speckle British Columbia's plateau culture area and other parts of the province. Through the regional "tellings," these stones (such as coyote stones) are commonly given human characteristics in the same way that certain animals are attributed with human properties and thus, ascribed with personhood (Scott 1989). Coastal and interior Salish peoples of British Columbia perceive rocks to be transformed people and have given them names (Mohs 1987; Teit 1900). Mountains, for both coastal and interior tribes of British Columbia, are ascribed special animate properties, are addressed by name and talked and prayed to. The Stó:lō people of coastal B.C. identify their mountains with the quality of *si:li*, meaning "my grandparents" (Archibald, in Bierwert 1999: 64). These attributions of personhood to non-human agents represent an experience of enfoldment, or imbrication, which Aboriginal people have with their territorial surroundings and its non-human agents. The sense of inhering within a shared niche, the connectivity of touch and the imbrication of the body with its world (as its sentient surrounds) collectively impart a spiritual unity between humans and non-humans, which thus animates the environment in a spiritually charged way.

Storyscape

The concept of "storyscape" addresses the issue of world emergence and speaks to the manner in which folkloric Aboriginal worlds are established, narratively, at the level of bodily travels. First Nations people have created and maintained their worlds through passing along their oral representations of ancestral travels dating back to early times and on the basis of their corporeal occupations within a territorial dwelling or shared landscape. The concept of "storyscape," thus, speaks to the manner in which Aboriginal being or selfhood within a place, as the imbrication of body and world, gets narratively encoded. This offers a locally recognizable, folkloric ordering of the world and the self's possibility. The concept of "storyscape" is useful, in light of the folklore under study, because it demonstrates how the territory of a particular people becomes personalized within narratives that depict their collective life story. The storyscape establishes the regional context of a people's social and environmental interaction and provides the foundation of their territorial self-identification. Thus, the lives and occupations of any given group of territorial dwellers, being regionally based, are understood and identified within environmental storyscapes (Stoffle, Halmo and Austin 1995: 6). It has been discovered that Native groups from all three culture areas (coastal, plateau and Athabaskan) of British Columbia identify a group of regional, territorial dwellers with a specific territorial landscape, which are folklorically designated in terms of a storyscape. In the case of the groups under study, the storyscapes that establish a people's self-identification within a territory occur on the basis of human activity and movement and ways of making a living within a place. They often reference what was done within a geographical region, such as a watershed or river delta, and tell about the various spots on the land that have been special sites of activity. In the case of body-world imbrication at a meaningful place of doing (such as a fishing site or berry picking patch) the nodal points of what has become a social and human world are encoded through folkloric, narrative depictions; they become embedded within a storyscape — the people's cultural memory. The stories of travels of pre-human ancestors and deities are formative in the folkloric depiction for many of the Aboriginal groups in British Columbia, because they set out the significant hunting grounds, fishing sites, resting spots, territorial markers and so on. Such storyscapes furnish a meaningful map, at the level of epic narratives, which speaks to the enfoldment of body and world in the non-dualistic sense. The lived world, as it is travelled on a daily basis, becomes the realized testimony and illustration of the stories told by the storytellers. Each sacred place or landmark is carefully referenced within the context stories, with reflexive legitimating statements[4] such as "it all happened right over there upon that very place," which is then meticulously described according to its physical characteristics. As a result, the land gets encoded into a territorial system of human meaning, on an epic or folkloric scale, and is a primary aspect of the collective selfhood and identity of the people. Thus, through the process of oral tradition and storytelling, the land and people's actions upon it get encoded into the cultural memory and identity of the region. The cultural meaning encapsulated in the folklore and passed along through the ancestral stories commonly embraces both the human and non-human agents of a shared landscape.

Poiesis

The concept of "*poiesis*" speaks to the most abstract level, that of the self's symbolic expression and presencing. It speaks to the many thematic representations that express the enfoldment of body and world as they are encoded in the narratives, or storyscapes, and inform and perpetuate the experience of the extended self at a cultural level. *Poiesis* refers to the many thematic and artistic representations that speak to the self's presencing within a territorial surrounds. Such environmental themes, or symbolizations, of personal and spiritual importance can be seen throughout the Native artwork of British Columbia, with its many environmental motifs from the traditional tribal territories. Other examples of environmental thematizations are the dramatizations present in dances which describe interactions with animals, for example, the Kwakwakawakw Hamatsa Dance, which recounts the story of the Great Cannibal Bird who lives at the North end of the world, and the coastal masks, for example, sun masks and moon masks. Totem poles that depict stories of the experiences of ancestors on the territory, where encounters with animals have carried a special significance, are also fitting examples. The term "*poiesis*" designates the self's expression of place in all of its multifarious and diverse forms. *Poiesis*, in sum, is the expressive form that represents the synthesis of body and world. This book on First Nations' connection to place acknowledges that there exists an Aboriginal poetics that demonstrates the existence of tribal territories as meaningful terrains of selfhood. Through a look at the multitude of First Nations' symbolic and poetic territorial art works and spiritual themes, tribal territories throughout British Columbia can be phenomenologically identified as ancient regions of human dwelling and activity and as areas of an unbroken enfoldment between the self and its surrounds.

The poetics of place, or a territory's *poiesis*, speaks ultimately to the ancestral and human events that define the territory. It is these ancestral events on the land that get passed down through poetic and artistic means and that ramify within a people as their collective identity. It is thus constitutive of that which is — environmentally speaking — their own. The poetics of dwelling, in the First Nations sense, can take the form of territorially specific stories, songs, dances based on territorial legends about the land, speech forms, family crests, regalia, rituals, masks, sacred objects and sacred places that retain the meaning and significance of the self's presencing while it occupies the land. Aboriginal expressive forms, as in the self's *poiesis* are the meaningful speaking out of the extended body's relationship to the world, as the environmental context of dwelling. They speak to the self's expansiveness and provide a vehicle for it to be communicated and borne forth. They create an aesthetic space for the self's realization in the extended sense, in terms of the ethos of real dwelling as meaningful existence.

An example is the way in which the body-word nexus, as a sonic articulatory phenomenon, generates a *poiesis* within Nlaka'pamux Stein Valley place names. Names as vivid, visual, sonic and kinesthetic descriptions of a significant place (i.e., what it feels like or sounds like to be there) give testimony to the body-world contexture and to the degree in which the landscape is self-defining. Similarly, a corresponding poetics of sound gestures can work together with the tactile sensuousness of the earth's slope to demonstrate how special named places on the tribal territory speak directly to the experience and presence of humans at that place. Sounds and feelings that are recorded by special named places are clear demonstrations of an embodied, cultural remembering. For this reason, articulatory phonetics, such as onomatopoeia, becomes the mimetic symbolizing of body and world in sonic and phonetic terms. In this same sense, extended bodily surfaces, as they are expressed poetically and narratively for many First Nations groups, result in an oral description of the landscape as anatomical parts, such as the Nlaka'pamux expression of a mountainside at the confluence of the Thompson and Fraser Rivers as a sleeping woman. The landscape becomes animated and personified as an environment that is neither external nor inert but rather speaks intimately to one's own bodily travels as sensuous selfhood.

In the case of the First Nations hunter-gatherers of British Columbia, the poetics of tribal territory and dwelling is evident throughout the region and manifests in a wide variety of aesthetic, narrative, symbolic and sonic articulatory forms. This poetics of First Nations territorial activity invariably demonstrates the nature of human and non-human enfoldment and a true sense of territorial belonging. The notion of territorial belonging, which suggests a sensuous body-world imbrication and its resultant expressiveness, is discussed at length above. In the case of British Columbia's Aboriginal peoples, both coastal and interior, formative components of meaning and identity flow from special sites on the land that remember place-based ancestral and human events and which bear identifying significance to the territorial dwellers. It is strongly borne out in the literature on coastal and interior narratives, rituals and traditions that the network of places originally linked together by the pathways of the ancestors' travels are, at the same time, a network or pathway of personal relations, such as territorial ownership. Moreover, they could represent tribal territorial behaviours (such as hunting, fishing and gathering patterns) or they could signify spiritual rights. These pathways, as given in the folk narratives, speak to the age-old territorial use patterns and sharing behaviours within a commonly held landscape or tribal territory which particular, well-known, inter-generational familial, ancestral groups call home.

For both coastal and interior peoples of British Columbia, the articulating and defining of landscape as the spiritual *poiesis* of their self-identification proves to be a primary feature within the oral traditions of the people, as seen in the supernaturally ascribed voice of the oral narratives and other folkloric and traditional forms. Characteristically, legends and ritual traditions are literally contextualized geographically in terms of important, well-known, oft-used, geographically marked places within the tribal territory that either signify a lineage's exact terrestrial origin — as seen in coastal tribes, such as the Gitxan (Cove 1987a), the Kwageulth or Kwakwakawakw (Goldman 1975) and the Stó:lō (Mohs 1987) — or map out the territory on the basis of age-old, ancestral use patterns, as is frequently seen in the in the case of interior groups (Teit 1900). The feelings about these places and the activities that took place there give rise to the many songs, dances, crests, symbols, narratives, ancient landmarks, aesthetic forms and place names that can be called a territorial poetics. The territorial *poiesis* which can be associated with a particular storyscape, or regional landscape that can be called a tribal territory, for the First Nations of British Columbia, is always based on what has happened there, in a feelingful, nostalgic, moral and ancestral sense that has placed people situationally and thematically within a background they call home.

As can be seen in Keith Basso's (1996) studies of the Western Apache, a phenomenon of place-based cultures is that their meaning systems are embedded in a well-known, oft-repeated poetics of place, with its embedded moral character communicated through stories. For the Aboriginal peoples of British Columbia also, the recognition of Aboriginal storyscapes set within the regional watershed landscapes, with their unique compendium of "ecoscapes" (Stoffle, Halmo and Austin 1995), as sites of bodily and narrative significance, become the most compelling tool available to achieve the double-edged purpose of territorial and Aboriginal preservation. Such stories map out meaningful, territorial dimensions by defining and depicting the land as an implicit and sacrosanct Aboriginal resource, not in terms of its mere utilitarian value nor its material worth but rather in terms of its sacred value and its true human value — its *poiesis*. The regional landscape as a storyscape and its corresponding *poiesis* of body and world, furthermore, provide more than just a topographical mapping with its itinerary of known places. Rather, it generates a web of human poetics as self-identification, cultural memory, narrative, a moral universe and the most intimate self-defining moments of a people. In fact, all of the articulations of Aboriginal possibilities stated above (and taken up throughout this text) can be sketched onto an activational, world-making continuum that depicts the life-defining moments and aspirations of the Native people themselves, as they have been dreamt and felt from ancient times. The perspective of a phenomenological *poiesis* as storyscape provides the chance to look at the activities and meanings of a people within the context of a land-based culture, while emphasizing their own diachronical[5] (progression and change) meaning of selfhood from the perspective of self, body and world.

The Concept of *Poiesis*

The concept of "*poiesis*" was originally given to us by Aristotle to look at the appeal and significance of Greek drama for the betterment of society. However, Heidegger transformed this concept to provide a concept of art that is important to the study of human spatiality. For Heidegger, unlike Aristotle, the artwork brings into presence, or manifests, the action of life itself and is not merely a mimesis of an already existent world. Heidegger's *poiesis* always represents artwork which is constitutive of a world and which serves the purpose of issuing forth the existence of a human space. Heidegger elaborates, therefore, that the positioning of an artwork in some sense marks out space in a sacrificial or sacred manner. In other words, the presence of artworks, or "*poiesis* (artistic production), consecrates a space whether it is out of doors or within a museum. Towering up within itself, the work opens up a world and keeps it abidingly in force" (Heidegger 1971c: 69). Thus, wherever an artwork sits, there is a world. By virtue of being a work, a work makes a space for spaciousness; it liberates the space of an open region and incorporates it into its structure. "To erect means: to open the right in the sense of a guiding measure, a form in which what is essential gives guidance" (69).

The power of artwork or *poiesis*, according to Heidegger, is what serves to gather the space and define it and, therefore, its force to create, anchor and bring forth the world. Thus, the notions of both belonging and being are vested in Heidegger's concept of *poiesis*. It is such a *poiesis* that opens up all spaces and worlds and consequently clears the way for human possibility upon the earth. By associating *poiesis* with world emergence, Heidegger analyzes the existence of a work of art with the creation of a place. It is the artwork that brings forth the place.

The emphasis on place that emerges from Heidegger's revision of Aristotle's concept of *poiesis* is taken in the direction of the human body by Maurice Merleau-Ponty. For Merleau-Ponty, the question of *poiesis*, or artistic expression, is explained in terms of the body's expressiveness, or its capacity to have its world as a world of sensorial meaning and experience. Unlike Aristotle and Heidegger, for whom *poiesis* refers to the activity of a single maker, Merleau-Ponty expands the notion to refer to innovative expressions of the body-world creation, of which all humans and humanity in general are involved.

Merleau-Ponty shows that all artistic and poetical expression is similar to authentic speech, or speech that is expressive of the actions of the lived body in relation to a phenomenal (sensorial) world, in which there is a relationship between "the sense being held within the word, and the word being the external existence of the sense" (1962: 182). In other words, in authentic speech the words directly express the human experience that gave rise to them. Language, if it is authentic, is strictly experiential. He argues that language and other forms of artistic expression are actually a "revelation of intimate being" and indicate the relationship between body and world:

> As soon as man uses language to establish a living relation with himself or with his fellows, language is no longer an instrument; it is a manifestation, a revelation of intimate being and of the psychic link which unites us to the world and our fellow men. (182)

Thus, for Merleau-Ponty, *poiesis* retains a strong gestural sense and emotional content in words, vowels and phonemes, which provide a means of "singing the world" directly. Language, in this instance, becomes a form of expressing the emotional content of a world. In the case of poetry or folklore, the meaning "swallows up" the symbols — or letters and words — to invoke a world context. *Poiesis* becomes the expression of a particular world as lived, which brings forth a particular world into view with all of its sensuous and emotional significances. *Poiesis* is the body's speaking out in its synergy with a surrounding world that it experiences sensuously and is able to express at the level of phonic or artistic gestures. Merleau-Ponty's conception focuses on

> the emotional content of the word, which we have called above all its "gestural" sense, which is all-important in poetry, for example. It would then be found that the words, vowels, and phonemes, are, so many ways of "singing the world" and that their function is to

represent things not, as naive onomatopoetic theory had it, by reason of an objective resemblance, but because they extract, and literally express their emotional essence. (187)

As in poetry, all language, according to Merleau-Ponty, expresses a position on the meaningful world as experienced through the senses, and this same concept can be adapted to Aboriginal folklore. A phonetic gesture, therefore, occasions for both speaker and hearer a particular expression of experience exactly as a body-world relationship would allow. As has been noted, it is through the expressive process that the body opens itself to an innovative pattern of behaviour that makes it understood to an external witness through a gesture. Such expressions occur, and are intelligible, according to the behavioural synthesis of body and world.

> The word and speech must somehow cease to be a way of designating things and thoughts, and become the presence of that thought in the phenomenal world and, moreover, not its clothing, but its token or its body. (182)

It is this power of human expression to invoke a sensory world that makes expression of any kind — artistic or otherwise — meaningful and communicative. For example, a spectator joins in on a theatrical performance with a knowledge and acceptance that precedes the intellectual working out of the play's meaning. "I become involved with things with my body; they co-exist with me as an incarnate subject" (187). It is enough that external space, a body and a field of action already exist as a surrounding field for the audience members to allow her to grasp the play and, therefore, the lived texture of another's everyday life. Every word (and its modulation) occupies a certain place within one's embodied world such that communication is possible.

For Merleau-Ponty, the arts such as music, speech, painting and literature cannot be reduced to their elements, such as the mere notes or colours or words. Rather, these idioms gain their true significance as arts in reference to an expressive and sensory world, to be experienced and understood by an audience at the level of the body's meaning. As in the case of Heidegger's *poiesis*, Merleau-Ponty also brings forth an environing world.

> it brings it to life in an organism of words, establishing it in the writer or the reader as a new sense organ, opening a new field or a new dimension to our experience. This power of expression is well known in the arts; for example, in music. The musical meaning of a sonata is inseparable from the sounds which are its vehicle: before we have heard it no analysis enables us to anticipate it; once the performance is over, we shall, in our intellectual analyses of music,

> be unable to do anything but carry ourselves back to the moment
> of experiencing it. (182)

Expression and artistic gestures of all kinds embody an experiential world and thus, open up a corresponding world of experience in the perception of the spectator or listener.

It is equally the case that, embedded within the firmament of a natural or geographic world (as in a First Nations territory), a human world and an emotional world are also present as a result of oral accounts, songs and other artistic gestures, which then allow the situational landscape in question to be noticed and experienced as a meaningful world. The various phonic and artistic gestures that result from behavioural patterns on the land contain the meaning and significance of the landscape. They provide the context and open up and hold in place the emotive and human world. Consequently, songs, mythologized landmarks, stories, poems, dances and other aesthetic gestures can be seen as poetic gestures, or "ways of singing the world" of human and non-human interaction. Such poetic gestures both set the space and open up a world and provide a meaningful context for human life. Several different uses of the term *poiesis* within anthropological literature extend Heidegger's and Merleau-Ponty's notions of a generically human capacity for *poiesis*. Oral tradition is a body-world synthesis in which *poiesis* becomes a collective creation.

Two current phenomenological writers, Steven Feld and Miriam Kahn, offer analyses of expression that supplement Merleau-Ponty's theories of body and world. Both writers discuss certain tribal people's approach to oral expressions that occur while living upon, identifying and speaking about the habitat.

Feld has employed the term *poiesis* interchangeably with his central concept of "poetics of place." For Feld, *poiesis* represents the various aesthetic, iconic forms of expression that "unite experiential realities of place to its expressive evocation" (1996a: 101). In Feld's interpretation, *poiesis* is the means by which sensuous experiential moments are connected to places through evocative, expressive, acoustic gestures, such as songs, or phonetic gestures. For example, according to Feld, the communication and poetic expression of the Kaluli people (of Papua New Guinea) is strongly auditory in nature, thus signifying and gesturing a sonic, articulatory world. As their language form emerges in the highly auditory environment of a densely forested regional habitat, it reflects the body-world synthesis typical of that place. An acoustemology within a forest habitat, Feld argues, is gestured and expressed in the many syllabic and sonic expressions that typify a people's regionally based experience. Indeed, Feld summarizes his "poetics of place" as the "the ways in which the Kaluli people encounter, sense and name places in their world and then to the ways this flow of world sensing turns into a sensual *poiesis* of place" (1996a: 101).

Miriam Kahn, in her studies of the New Guinea Wamiran (1996), argues for an emotional and expressive relationship between a people's landscape and tribal traditions. In Kahn's ethnographic study, "history in general is described in terms of relationships between migrations, myths, names, and localities that are recalled in songs, stories, and ritual" (1996: 193). Kahn explains how various landmarks and stories embody the emotional value of the landscape, which acquires its significance on the basis of what happened there and "provides tangible forms for the mooring of memory":

> History, biography, memory, and emotion all merged with and settled in the landscape. The places would trigger strong emotions for Wamirans after I had left, because they would be all that Wamirans had as reminders of me. In discussing how places with strong emotional content often evoke loss, Steven Feld (this volume) says that "living far away one is deeply reminded of places as kin; path connections are like familiar places calling back to you." (188)

My intention is to demonstrate how elements of mimesis, emotion and expression first delineated by Aristotle have been amplified by the focus on place in Heidegger, body in Merleau-Ponty and finally extended into the collective body of oral tradition by contemporary anthropological writers. In both Aristotle and Heidegger, *poiesis* is an artistic process that emerges from, and expresses, an arena of human life. Heidegger's phenomenological discussions on the non-duality and spatiality of an artwork are extended by Merleau-Ponty to explain the ability of artistic and poetic expression to "open up a world" for human experience. Thus, the terms "poetics" and "*poiesis*" are used throughout this book as a means of demonstrating the body-world synthesis as argued within European phenomenology. Heidegger's conceptualization of an artwork as bringing forth a world through the spaciousness of its own being and presence provides a clue to how First Nations folklore opens up a human world within a natural geographic one, thus making human habitation possible and meaningful. Merleau-Ponty's conceptualization of poetry and art as having an emotive content (as linked to gestures) gives further insight into how poetic and artistic gestures of all kinds open up a world, in correspondence with our own behavioural patterns and bodily experience. The term "*poiesis*," therefore, is useful in explaining the role of stories, songs, mythological landmarks and various traditions practised on the land by the diverse First Nations within British Columbia. *Poiesis* conceptualizes the relationship between the land's human/emotional value and the resultant spatial thematizations, such as oral gestures, traditional landmarks and other forms of artistic or aesthetic production (such as commemorative poles or crests) that give rise to order and sustain the territorial world. Such a concept provides emphasis on the manner in which the body has its world, and how this world is communicated, experienced and passed along through a continuum of traditional gestures, oral traditions and creative artistic works.

The term *"poiesis"* is employed to conceptualize the link between human expression and everyday experience. In this case, the term highlights the creative gestures within the world as the result of heartfelt, emotive and sensual experiences, and thus as emanations of the experience of place. *Poiesis* is employed to demonstrate how the Aboriginal traditions of the various territorial groups relate to, express, open-up and sustain the world, as Merleau-Ponty describes it, for human habitation and doing. Poetic manifestations, such as oral expressions and poetic gestures, arise from sensual experiences, such as food-getting and migratory practices and travels from place to place. In my usage, *poiesis* conceptualizes the relationship between the land's emotional value and the resultant spatial thematizations, such as landmarks, rock art sites, oral gestures and songs. Phenomenological theory provides emphasis on the manner in which the body has its world and how this world is communicated, experienced and perpetuated through a continuum of traditional gestures, oral traditions and spatial thematizations, such as sacred landmarks.

Throughout this book I illustrate the importance of a tribal territory as a "field of self," as opposed to a mere domain of economic advantage, as is generally suggested in Eurocentric thinking. By describing folkloric representations, I show that First Nations people living within British Columbia have an emotional and spiritual connection to their landscapes which relates to their deepest definition of self. This work illustrates the fit between the phenomenological analysis of selfhood and the folkloric perspectives. To this end, I apply the concepts of "enfoldment," "storyscape" and *"poiesis"* to demonstrate how Aboriginal communicative and symbolic vehicles offer a holistic view of personhood and the extended self. This is in contrast to the typical European Cartesian view of self (as homo economicus) that serves as the foundation of the legal discourse of land claims. The chapter demonstrates how tribal territories in British Columbia offer stories and aesthetic iconography (such as songs, dances, carved poles, masks, crests, landmarks, rock art, etc.) as statements on the First Nations people as being both imbricated and self-identified with a territorial surrounds, as terrestrial dwelling places. Such forms indicate the presence of a territorial *poiesis* that is self-defining for the people of each region. Examples of such storyscapes are the Stein Valley for the Nlaka'pamux people and the Lillooet River drainage area for the Statliumx people. Both of these storyscapes are discussed in order to illustrate the importance of the territory for the First Nations people and the corresponding relationship of self, body and world. A similar profile is evident in the storyscapes of coastal culture groups, such as the Stó:lō, the

Taku Tlingit, the Kwakwakawakw, the Gitxan and the Nuu-chah-nulth. Throughout the folkloric representations specific to these people, the spiritual and artistic iconography that abounds speaks to the enfoldment of body, self and territory in a manner that can be summed up as a territorial *poiesis*.

Notes

1. Ground-truthing is a research method whereby elders draw out in pencil on a topographical map of their tribal territory all the places they have used for Aboriginal practices over their lifetime.

2. "Authentic dwelling" is a term borrowed from Heidegger that refers to an authenticity of life, whereby meaning and values are derived from direct practice and through the experience of being in and caring for a place.

3. The term "whitestream" is used to indicate the difference between First Nations people and the rest of the Canadian citizenry who are non-Native and who are not administered under the *Indian Act*. For most of Canada's history, up to the present, the majority of the non-Native population in most parts of Canada is of European ancestry.

4. A "reflexive legitimating statement" is one that reflects on an historical event, thus giving a souvenir and proof of its having occurred. Thus the transformer stories, for coast and interior Salish, are shown as territorial landmarks that orally record and stand for events that took place in ancestral time.

5. "Diachronic" is a term borrowed from French anthropologist Claude Levi-Strauss that refers to the process of change as opposed to the condition of remaining static.

Chapter 4

Poetics and Stories
among Coastal First Nations

> You usually have to speak to these places to let them know that
> you're not a stranger. Otherwise, the power in the place may make
> strange upon you.... These places are special. (Stó:lō elder EP, in
> Mohs 1987: 87)

The previous chapter describes the hunter-gatherer experience (as represented in the Aboriginal folklore of the people of British Columbia)
as holistic, in contrast to the norm in Western rationalist, Cartesian, thinking, with its emphasis on the mind being separate from the body. Societies
founded on a subject-object opposition, which oppose self and world, nature
and culture, human and non-human, and self and other as their dominant
ontological foundation, see nature as inanimate and external and emotionally separate from the self. Such rationalist views, found commonly within
European originated societies, construct a bifurcated reality based on oppos-
ing categories: starting with the dichotomy between the categories of subject
and object, as popularized in the procedures of modern science. This chapter
demonstrates the more imbricated experience of human selfhood within the
First Nations people of British Columbia, who since ancestral time have
been self-identified with and ontologically inseparable from their territories.

In the sense that hunters and fishers interact continuously and closely
with the non-human beings and processes of their environment, they experience selfhood as one which flows together in an unbroken continuity
with the non-human world. For example, as a hunter-gather every stage
of my humanity is set against the background of the environing earth that
my people engage with. Thus, it is experienced as a perpetual meshing of
gears between human cycles and the other earthly cycles such as the seasons
(Goldman 1975). Although the fabric of hunter-gatherer life is not identical
with these surrounding earthly processes, the experience of self is strongly
identified with them.

In the following chapters, the disclosures about Aboriginal territory focus
on the self as an experiential field, as opposed to an enclosed, alienated or

atomized self. Aboriginal territory is the capsule of embodied activities on the land and is the container for all the aesthetic and folkloric expressions that pertain to it. The storied environmental surrounds signify the people's experiences and their ongoing relationship with both animate and inanimate entities that share the same terrestrial world with the people (Evernden 1985; Ingold 1996; Merleau-Ponty 1968).

It is the many journeys over the land undertaken by the First Nations of British Columbia, within their respective storyscapes, that give definition to the world, which has become understandable within an activational context. It is the "tellings" on the land that are the wellspring of First Nations' identity and culture, and that also form a collective meaning system which has always bound the community together (Merleau-Ponty). The meaningful self thus arises through an existential process of emergence — through a journeying throughout the territory. It is the journeys that serve to orientate a person within the universe of all other entities and people that are encountered. In this case, human spatiality can be described as an interior "living map" of human experiences that serve both to guide and to situate the human self. Thus, human spatiality and selfhood is accumulated through contact with all of that which one has had a familiarity with and dwelled beside.

> The "environment" does not arrange itself in a space which has been given in advance; but its specific world-hood, in its significance, articulates the context of involvements which belongs to some current totality of circumspectively allotted places. The world at such a time always reveals the spatiality of the space which belongs to. (Heidegger 1962: 138)

A folkloric depiction of self as one flowing together with the non-human world offers a challenging and revolutionary view (philosophically and environmentally) compared to the modern mainstream "whitestream" perspective. In both the coastal and interior narrative traditions, references to the spirit beings on the land and the animal hunters in the bush show that First Nations peoples have interacted with the non-human processes of their environment in a familiar and connected way (Feit 1995). This suggests a more intimate view of the surrounding natural world than is characteristically found within whitestream perspectives and illustrates a greater degree of imbrication between humans and the natural world.

The writings of Maurice Merleau-Ponty offer a clue on how meaning originates from the body's movements in space as they are built up as habits and activities incorporated inside our body as "body image" or stored experiences. The respect and self-identification that First Nations people demonstrate for their territories can be summed up as a lived attachment to them and a heartfelt concern for them as their own "embodiment." A person makes sense out of the world within a human landscape on the basis of all of the stories that have been handed down over the generations. The territory, as a body-world matrix which has been dreamt and thematized (mapped out and captured in art), becomes the focal point for all cultural and aesthetic expressions (Zaner 1981: 171; Merleau-Ponty 1962; Feld 1996b; Elsey 2001).

Poetic and folkloric representations, expressive of the territory within First Nations stories, thus represent a human geography — what might be termed a "sacred landscape"[1] of human involvement (Stoffle, Halmo and Austin 1995). The geological formations (such as, interesting rocks and prominent mountains) in British Columbia's First Nations territories are often talked about as being people and have been given a poetic identity in that they express people's feelings about themselves and the land. An abundance of poetic explanations can also be found for the animal beings who (as we are told by Colin Scott, Tim Ingold and others) share a place in the same habitat and process of survival and communicative reality as humans — they all interact together (Scott 1989: 130). Words, syllables, songs, landmarks, place names and ritual behaviours can be seen as the poetic representation of a wider environing life world of both human and non-human participants, within a territorial dwelling (Abram 1996, Zaner 1981).

Such a perspective has been useful, for example, in situating the creation stories of the Yenyedi people on the Taku River, the folklore of Mount Cheam for the Stó:lō people and the travels of the Transformers in the folkloric traditions of the Stl'atl'imx' and the Nlaka'pamux plateau peoples. The *poiesis* found in the ethnographic literature is expressive of the relationship between body and world as a behavioural setting.

Self, Body and World
among Coastal First Nations

For the coastal people of British Columbia, as well as non-coastal groups, the defining and articulating of landscape and special places is a primary feature of self-identification, both as seen within the oral tradition and as reflected in the hereditary rights of families within regional storyscapes. Characteristically, names, crests, legends and territorial rights are contextualized geographically with respect to important marked places within the territory. For example, descriptions in the folklore of the coast Salish refer to many large stone beacons that have become mythological sites of self-identification, plus territorial markers for the people of a specific hereditary territory (Mohs 1987).

The coast Salish people of the Fraser River region, the Halq'eméylem speaking and the Stó:lō people (or River People) possess a mythic tradition that is founded on the ways of supernatural transformers, which is also characteristic to Salish speakers elsewhere in the province. For the coastal Halq'eméylem speakers, such as the Stó:lō, the creation of mythological landmarks (deemed to be sacred places) is largely, although not exclusively, attributed to the transformer Xa:ls, who put the physical world in order and rid the land of dangerous beings and whose "place in Stó:lō cosmology and in Stó:lō culture history cannot be overstated" (Mohs 1987: 88). These Xa:ls creation stories can be associated with a large number of storied places, storied landmarks and transformer stones within the Stó:lō territory.

The colourful story of Xeyxelemos is an example of the activities at a place being sealed within a landform. The transformer rock Xeyxelemos, near a fishing site that belongs to a Stó:lō person by the name of Sweetie Malloway, is indeed a container for dynamic movement, meaning and change, such as is implied in the term *"poiesis."* "The container image places the unseen, rocky river bed at the base, and the rest of the dynamics as occupants" (Bierwert 1999: 44). At each fishing site, the canyon yields a vortex of fishly performance whirling through it, into which corresponding human performers extend their technologies while their mythic, social and poetic worlds spiral out.

The place is the repository of memories, of dangers and of loss of lives within the river canyon. It is a primary stage for the drama of human activity and survival that is central to lives of the coastal people. It combines both human and natural energies in such a way that it has served as a primary form of sustenance for an entire people until today, and provides an ethos of identity and self — shown in the determination to carry on in the face of obstacles that can seldom be matched in tenacity by any group. According to Bierwert, Sweetie's stories include many memories and dramas, although she tells us that the simple good feeling for the place is her primary reason for being there. "Some years there have been conflicts, once about another family's claim to a fishing site, and often the implicit conflict of interest with saltwater commercial fishermen whenever the salmon runs do not make it back into the rivers in large numbers" (49).

Salmon work on the river, with its wind-drying fish camps, drying racks of salmon, cabins and fish shelters make visible the social fabric of Stó:lō family relations and their cooperative practices. A family of a single mother, for example, with sons, worked a fishing site until they were grown men. Her sons grew up hauling fish for their family. It is obvious that on the river people recreate and re-establish their working ties over and over again.

Life at the mythic place Xeyxelemos, near Sweetie's camp, shows the features of life and work, which continually add depth and significance to the historical dimension and the meaning of place.

A dry rack has a permanent frame and roof, but no sides, with poles to hang filleted fish under shelter in the event of rain. The fish dries coppery and luminous in about ten days, stiff with a concentrated flavour; not smoked, but pure salmon — like nothing else in the world. The cabins have bunks for people to sleep on, boxes for cupboards as storage and a cooking area for daily meal preparation and sometimes for canning fish during a regular opening. Some camps have cleared areas for little children to play in. Fish-dry camps are a haven for the people, where ancient technologies of wind-drying salmon coexist with the best outboard motors people can afford, and with techniques of gill-netting that are fixed by the government regulations first established in 1907.

According to Bierwert, each moment on the river (and each fishing-set) is carefully watchful, as at all times the river's bounty is framed with dangers. Men lose their lives practically every year if they happen to read the river's signs badly. Especially around Sweetie's camp are the waters particularly turbulent. All of this is presided over by "Lady Franklin's Rock," Xeyxelemos, whose story stands testimony to the meaningful absorption within a place. Such absorption is made obvious in the swirl of activity at Sweetie's camp, while the landmark provides the poetic embodiment of the immanent forces and dangers there, and how they are experienced:

> As we sit at her fishing place in 1992, Sweetie tells me, "there used to be an old Indian doctor there," gesturing at the rock. "He was killing people with his power. So they put him there; he's in the rock. You can still see him, his eye." She projects effectively when she tells of this particular presence, and I feel both awed and discomfited by it, a bit taken aback because I have marvelled at the rock before, even imagined the adventure of trying to cross over to it and walk around among the cedars on top of it. (54–55)

Sweetie's story implies an assumed knowledge on our part about the Salish mythic tradition of the transformer Xa:ls, mentioned above. Xa:ls is the one who put the evil Indian doctor in the rock, and the story harkens back to a mythic period in ancestral time when a transformer, or group of transformers, made these kind of changes in the world, geographical changes that are perceivable by the people even today: "Transformer figure stories comprise part of a dispersed and episodic coast Salish mythic tradition, distinguishable from other stories because of what Transformers do: change a person into an animal or a feature of the landscape." Ethnographic accounts (Boas 1894; Hill-Tout 1904) indicate that Xa:ls first manifested at Harrison Lake and travelled the Salish territories in the disguise of a young bear and his brothers (also Dawson 1891 in Mohs, 1987, and Teit 1898, 1900, 1909, 1917). It wasn't until Xa:ls returned from Vancouver Island that he assumed a human form and then travelled up the Fraser River from Point Roberts, transforming and defining the landscape.

Mrs. Jim and Mr. George speak in Halq'eméylem (translated by Brent Galloway):

Mrs. Jim:	I wonder if it's Xelhalh she is talking about (when she refers to a place "above Yale")
Mr. George:	Yes.
Mrs. Jim:	Xeyxelemos was a taboo (sacred) person; there's nothing ...
Mr. George:	Just that you are on the other side, talking ...
Mrs. Jim:	You don't know anything.
	You are a fresh child, beside me.
	I know much.
	It's that I've forgotten it.
	They got there.
	The changing people got there.
	They were called transformers.
	That person (Xeyxelemos) — like a supernatural creature was winning.
	His eye is fixed.
	One of his eyes is over his neck.
	So the people (the transformers) started to look.
	They went inside the house and then started to become laid out (stiffen, lose consciousness).
	You just don't look in the inside of his house.
Mr. George:	Is that Xeyxelemos?
Mrs. Jim:	Yes.
	I got to the third time he was approached, and now he was beaten and so became a rock.
Wells:	What does she say?
Mrs. Cooper:	What does she mean Xeyxelemos?
Mr. George:	Oh, this guy from ...
Mrs. Jim:	The name of the one from Xelhalh, who was changed; then he became a rock.
Mrs. Cooper:	Where's Xelhalh?
Mr. George:	The other side of Yale, on this end of the tunnel.
	Yeah, there's a man there owned the place, and nobody go in there.
Mrs. Jim:	There's nobody that ordered him around when only he lived there.

(Wells 1987, in Bierwert 1999: 57)

All accounts of Xeyxelemos relate to the power of the place. In fact, Xeyxelemos is so powerful that he had to be confronted three times before he was vanquished. Both accounts — Sweetie's and Mrs. Jim's — one authoritative and historical, the other remembered from immediate experience, draw attention to the danger of the rock and the dauntingness of the place's power. The stories speak of latent activity within this stone, which illustrates a power "once animated" but now fixed in stone to mark the site, as though reminiscing on the timeless vortex of age-old human activity and its accompanying dangers as they are enfolded within that niche.

Demonstrated clearly within the discussion above are that such landmarks and places have an animate nature and reflect "what is done there." The rock represents the body-world synthesis of the events that unfolded at that place. A member of the Stó:lō First Nation, Joanne Archibald (founder of the Curriculum Development Project and currently director of the University of British Columbia First Nations' House of Learning) gives deeper cogency to the idea that non-human agents can be animated in terms of human doings, or in other words, have personhood. She recalls one of her elders speaking about some parts of nature as being her *si:li*: "The mountains are your *si:li*. That's our word for grandparents; *si:li*. You have to respect them. You have to respect your grandparents" (64). Another women contributes: "All living things they are all *si:li*. And the rocks too, even the little rocks. Everything there is *si:li*, to be respected." Following this disclosure, several other women explained to Bierwert that *si:li* is generally present within a story, and when one is asked to adopt a prayerful respect and acknowledgment when travelling or harvesting on a mountain, or seeking comfort or receiving purification from a river or cedar trees. Such accounts demonstrate how the mountain, as *si:li*, expresses one's identity as a field of human doing in the extended sense, thus depicting human activity as also enfolding non-human features of the wider environment and territory.

Wilson Duff (1952) notes the importance of Mt. Cheam as a bear, deer and mountain goat hunting ground. It is also known that Stó:lō women made trips once a year to Mt. Cheam in order to collect numerous types of wild berries as well as molten mountain goat wool, used in weaving (interview material in Mohs 1987: 96). At one time, Mt. Cheam was also a site for the acquisition of salt (Mohs 1987: 96). In addition, flint was quarried from a stream that flows down the south side of the mountain (William Sepass in Jenness 1934/35 in Mohs 1987: 96). Several families claim a special relationship to Mt. Cheam "as a mountain goat hunting site," noted by Boas (1894), Jenness (1934/35), and recently in a Coqualeetza publication. These sources claim that Mt. Cheam is the original home of the Mt. Cheam Goat People. Boas writes:

> The Pa'pk'um (popkum). Their ancestor was called Aiuwa'luQ,
> When Quals met him, he transformed him into a mountain goat.
> This is why there are so many mountain goats on tle'tlEk.e mountain
> to the southwest of Pa'pk'um. (1895: 40, in Mohs 1987: 97)

It is believed that Aiuwalux's descendants departed from their mountain home, and, taking on human form, they intermarried with the Cheam people, who now profess their ancestral relationship to them. Furthermore, conservation and health of the goat population on Mt. Cheam continues to be the concern of these legendary families, along with the other Stó:lō people, further illustrating the notion of *si:li:*

> Long ago a multitude of mountain goats came down from Cheam Mt. and changed to people. They are the ancestors of the Sepass family. Hence the Sepass family have the right to paint a goat on their coffin. (Jenness 1934/35, in Mohs 1987: 97)

The Cheam highlands represent one of the few sacred mountainous sites in the Stó:lō territory. Another and different tale tells us that Mt. Cheam is a mother (being the front-most peak) who, along with her daughter and her dog, was changed into a mountain. This transformation occurred after she left her husband Kwxa:lxw, who is known as Mt. Baker, in Washington State. Mohs tells us that the varying stories can be understood on the basis of geographical proximity, demonstrating how poetic representations of landscape, in relationship to the thematization of alternating figures within a background, relate to body and world and the changing visual orientations of people at different points of the territory (Elsey 2001: Chapter 3 and 4).[2] The sisters on Cheam Ridge, for example, dominate the skyline when looking at Mt. Cheam from Katzie in the east. However, the mother and her daughters are an outstanding sight when seen from Seabird Island, in the north. Moreover, Lhilheqey and her dog prevail when viewed from the west, near Chilliwack and Mission. The poetics of each view, as in the phenomenological concept of world as a "ratio of the senses," responds to the given body-world matrix within a particular vantage point and represent a given combination of activity and perception as it is lived and felt in the lives of the local people. The activational poetics of human involvement is captured in the following quotation on the mountain's meaning as grounded reality: "You could learn more of Stó:lō spirituality by spending a few nights down here by the river or up Mount Cheam. That will teach you more than we could ever tell you" (S.S.F. in Mohs 1987: 95–96).

The age-old connection and absorption of Stó:lō people with their territory at certain significant sites emerges in the manifestation of an iconic *poiesis* of humans and land, in the depictions of Mt. Cheam. This honouring of, and absorption with, the non-human world of the territorial surrounds are embedded in Stó:lō legends and are the foundation of their self-identification as a people, as depicted in the idea of the landscape as *si:li.* The Native names given to the various peaks and other geographical features stress the importance of the Cheam region. "The mountain lakes, two caves, and the creeks emanating from here all have Indian names. Some of these names are carried by living members of the Stó:lō Indian community" (Wells 1965, in Mohs 1987: 98). These names are passed on from generation to generation, further stressing the self-identification of the people with the territory as the intimate field of the extended self (Elsey 2001: 203–204, Chapter 3, section 3.3).

For the coastal Taku Tlingit, of Northern British Columbia, the defining and articulating of landscape and special places is a primary feature of self-identification, both as seen within the oral tradition and as reflected in the hereditary rights of families within regional storyscapes. Characteristically, names, crests, legends and also territorial rights are contextualized geographically with respect to important marked places within the territory. In the case of the Taku, a specific group of Tlingit, the hereditary names of the houses are said to come from the Taku River itself, as a way of keeping the association between Yanyedi people (owners of the river) and land visible through a system of matrilineal kinship, by which stories are handed down (Nyman and Leer 1993: 17–18). According to Thornton in his explorations of the Tlingit:

> An important but often overlooked aspect of Tlingit clans is their geographical basis. Two aspects of clan geography are particularly significant: origin and distribution. Origin refers to the location where the clan was founded as a distinct social group and is typically from where it derives its name. The majority of Tlingit clans adopted their names from specific places where they were formed. What is more, the linguistic construction of such clan names evokes a sense of belonging or being possessed by the names place. (Thornton 1997: 296)

In Atlin, the Taku Tlingit Wolf clan is called Yanyedi, and its territory is seen to be the Taku River. According to Taku Tlingit elder Mrs. Nyman, in her discussions on Taku Tlingit origins (Nyman and Leer 1993), territorial associations between people and land are embedded in stories about the river and the watershed wherein their fishing and hunting occur. In the stories of old Yanyedi, a mountain in the Taku River is seen as a heart, with an accompanying story about a heart ripped it out of a body and thrown on the land. In the Taku narrative about the formation of the landscape of the lower Taku River, two giants fought and in the ensuing struggle, one giant (which is now a mountain on one side of the river) ripped out the windpipe of the other giant and threw it onto the land. This place is marked by a landmark rock formation, where the wind howls past and is noted within the folklore to be the dead giant's windpipe. The giant lives on, however, in dismembered form as parts of the river and river valley — his parts are strewn throughout the territory. The heart of the giant was ripped out also and thrown into the Taku River; its location is now marked by a heart-shaped island (Nyman and Leer 1993: 17–18).

The Yanyedi people relate their name and origin to a location near where this titanic struggle took place, and thus the land gains personhood as the extended bodily surface of the Yanyedi. Each site of mythological significance represents the bodily incorporation and self-identification of the Yanyedi people with that site, through age-old schemes of bodily action and established patterns of territorial use of the river. The thematization of the river as a cultural icon opens up the space between the river and the surrounding geography for the purposes of the Yanyedi manifesting a folkloric *poiesis* (or storyscape) incorporating the articulation of landscape, social memory and the self-identification of the people within that place.

According to Cove (1982), Duff (1959), Goldman (1975) and others, territories are sacred to the families who own them. The territories are vested with a unique collection of tribal folklore and symbolism that explains their cultural background and genealogical origins. They are, furthermore, speckled with ancient mythic/historical landmarks and vision sites that speak to important and formative events that occurred there. According to Hudson, in the case of the Nisga'a of the Nass Valley, a system of ritual or traditional names "remain identified with tracts of land and resource areas, they provide a framework for enduring social relations and the Nisga'a land tenure system" (1987: 10). The basis of Tsimshian land tenure (Cove 1982; Duff 1959), as seen for the Gitxan, the Nisga'a and the Tsimshian, is a system of titles and houses. For example, there are approximately sixty-five houses or *wilps* (a Tsimshian term) among the four major Nisga'a villages. These houses have their territories in the vicinity of their respective villages and belong to four major clans or *pdeek*, namely Laxsgiik (Eagle), Laxgibuu (Wolf), Gisk'ahaast, or Gispuwudwada (Killer Whale, Grizzly Bear) and Ganada (Frog, Raven) (Hudson 1987: 4). Houses are consolidated as territorial units through common ancestry, shared traditions and symbols, songs, crests and dances. Moreover, in the case of the Tlingit, on the northern coast of British Columbia, Thornton (1997) and de Laguna (1972) demonstrate a similar profile as to how territory, geographical features and ritual personality are linked on the basis of house groups:

> Clans or their localized segments, known as house groups, owned and maintained use rights to physical property (including salmon streams, halibut banks, hunting grounds, sealing rocks, berrying grounds, shellfish beds, canoe-landing beaches, and other landmarks) as well as symbolic property (such as names, stories, songs, regalia, crests, and other cultural icons, including clan ancestors and representations of geographic features). These possessions (*at.*

oow) were integral components of Tlingit identity, and each clan was conceived of as having not only its exclusive property, but also its own unique "personality" and ways of being. (de Laguna 1972: 451, in Thornton 1997: 296)

Consequently, the argument can be made that, on the basis of a hereditary land-tenure system, there exists in perpetuity a folkloric, territorial union or *poiesis* (an iconography) of people and landscape that is seminal to the ritual and belief structure (selfhood) of the societies, on the basis of kinship and descent as conveyed through totemic symbolism. Therefore, as elaborated earlier, the selfhood of the people is merged with the land. Both non-human agents and the coastal First Nations together co-exist within (as Ingold explains it) a common "enfoldment of being" upon the land, as depicted within a regional *poiesis*, or folkloric personality of the various coastal storyscapes. I explore, by engaging with the world and its activities, how the coastal First Nations (within a continuous living present) have become immersed within their environmental surrounds. As a result, their selfhood has acquired thematic definition and a terrestrial articulation in response to a recognizable territorial background; the body and world relationship has been the foundation of this nexus.

A phenomenological approach argues that meanings are produced on the basis of lived bodily experiences. Consequently, the environmental surroundings (authentically speaking), in terms of what are perceived as traditional territories, are not merely an external out there, such as in a Cartesian model. Rather, it is a familiarized field activity and belongingness. A phenomenological analysis of coastal and interior Aboriginal peoples' relationship to the land, therefore, looks primarily at the land's specific meanings as a statement about Aboriginal self-identification within a territory. Creation stories, Aboriginal place names, important mythological landmarks and sites and other poetic, symbolic and aesthetic "representations" (such as songs, dances and crests) all serve as entry points to the land's meaningfulness as human possibility. In sum, people always understand the land in relationship to themselves and things that happened.

Storytelling and its accompanying rituals are the communicative nexus of dwelling as "being-in-the-world." It is the poetic and expressive vehicle of absorbed involvement with the world, both human and non-human, and reflects the "poetic" relationship of the performers (the First Nations people) with their ancestral lands and territories. The territory can be seen in terms of a topographical map or storyscape comprised of activity sites; whereby place names and important mythological markers — landmarks and story sites, for example — serve as age-old territorial markers or poles of action (or thematic anchors) that represent particular places of traditional land tenure (for example, within certain families) and of ancestral territorial use and meaning.

The Coastal First Nations Personality as Dwelling

To understand the framing of the coastal Aboriginal personality as "dwelling," as merged within a house group and territorial surrounding, one has to contextualize the role of the person as a house member alongside the imbrication of the house within a tribal territory. On this basis, the personality or selfhood of the individual is merged, in a type of enfoldment with the territory, by virtue of a self-identification and belonging to the house group and its symbolic *poiesis* — its stock of hereditary privileges, such as names and crests, which inform the identity and personhood of individuals living within the house. The household, according to Cove (1982) for the Gitxan, but also Duff (1959) for the Tsimshian and Nuu-chah-nulth and Goldman (1975) for the Kwageulth or Kwakwakawakw (profiles that reflect most coastal groups), is seen as an incredible source of physical and spiritual power, as it is believed to embody (or enfold) the power of the non-human agents that populate and represent the traditional territory of its ancestral belonging.

Tribal territorial practices, symbolism and stories, the symbolic *poiesis*, are contextualized within traditional territories that portray a complex nexus of practical activity and human doing. This is seen in the fact that the territories correspond to the watershed of a given salmon river or stream (including the entire drainage off the side of a mountain), plus the surrounding hunting land and the land that served as the root digging spots, foraging valleys, berry picking sites, sacred sites etc. We are told by Cove (1982) and Kirk (1986) that the determinant of tribal territories as hereditary units for coastal groups — the Gitxan or Tsimshian, for example — is found in the ecological reality of salmon availability and its accompanying value. Salmon's high density, its importance in trade and its seasonal predictability all determined that the salmon streams and inlets should dictate the location of territories (Cove 1982: 4). According to a number of sources (Barbeau and Beynon 1915–1956, in Cove 1987a, 1982; Halpin 1973), the average tribal territory, in the case of the Gitxan, for example, equals approximately two hundred square miles, to which they have proprietary rights, as in "the right to use or enjoy, the right to exclude others, and the right to alienate" (Cove 1982: 5).

In the case of the coastal tribes such as the Gitxan, the meaningful activities and movements of a closely related and relatively exclusive group on land determines what constitutes the house, or *wilp*, to use the Gitxan/Tsimshian word. A *wilp*, in other words, is a group of people living and working together on a selection of surrounding territory as its most fundamental determinant of meaning and belonging; it thus represents their "dwelling." The *wilp*'s primary function was to confer title over a territory to a corporate group on the basis of matrilineal descent and to connote the method of "traditional dwelling," which identified for example how house members dwelt alongside non-house members. This was accomplished by the house (through the enactment of a symbolic *poiesis*) at a traditional feast, where ritual songs, dances, names and crests expressive of the territory, were displayed to establish house members' title and territorial rights (Cove 1982: 6).

In sum, these aesthetic forms are a direct statement of the territory and the enfoldment of the Gitxan people within it. The Gitxan people then, in Aboriginal terms, have carried out their lives within *wilps*, which included fixed technologies, such as permanent fishing traps and weirs, and fishing sites, and had predictable and established settlement patterns within what could be referred to as a regional landscape, which is also a storyscape. The territorial rights of the *wilps* are thus established on the basis of a symbolic iconic *poiesis*, which is embedded in all the names, crests, regalia, folklore and dances that have become incorporated into articulatory space as expressions of body and world. In the previous chapter it was argued that a mythology not only presents to us a world but also interprets the experience of being in it. If we concentrate on the interpretive aspect, "Tsimshian texts can be seen as guides who take us where we wish to go in that world and teach us to understand what we discover there" (Cove 1987a: 49). The corresponding link between stories and world can be seen in the following paraphrase of Adams by Cove:

> Adams (1973: 21–37) provides the most comprehensive presentation of those units in his reconstruction of a typical pre-contact *Gitxan* village. He describes it as consisting of two major resident groups, called Sides, each made up of members from one of the four totemic divisions or clans (*pdek*) — Wolf, Eagle, Frog, and Fireweed. These are broken down into local sub-clans (*wilnad'ahl*) which share common myths about place of origin. They, in turn, are made up of corporate units known as houses (*wilp*). The ethnographic record tends to support that Houses were the principal territorial units. (Adams, in Cove 1982: 6)

Iconical *Poiesis* in Nuu-chah-nulth Whaling Culture

The symbolic/iconic expression of land and the integration of the human and the non-human world in ritual forms is similarly found in Wilson Duff's (1965) treatment of a Nuu-chah-nulth whaling canoe. The Nuu-chah-nulth live on the west coast of Vancouver Island close to the town of Tofino. Duff shows how the whaling canoe is suggestive of an iconic *poiesis* which imbricates the visual imagery, the social memory and an identification with place, all wrapped together in the designs and symbols of the Nuu-chah-nulth canoe. In Duff's treatment of the whaling canoe's iconography and symbolism, we are shown how the territorial iconography of the chief's family (such as that of the head chief of Ahousat, for example) is carried over into the designs, pigments and charms used on the whaling boat: "They concern magical beliefs and practices which were normally retained, as well-guarded family secrets" (Paul Sam, speaker for the Ahousat chief, in Duff 1965: 29).

It is significant that family houses always get their stock of ceremonial and ritual objects from the hereditary, tribal territory and its fishing region, and they are garnered from special magical places on the land. "The mixtures painted on the lines down the throat of the bow were made from secret formulas owned by families and chiefs and they varied with different tribes and different types of canoes" (29). Much of the ritual formula was apparently focused on the "scratch marks" down the sides of the boat. Those down the throat of the bow were said to be from a special mixture to quiet the whale; the ones painted down the stern were believed to quiet the sea. Others were to identify the ownership of the chief and to prevent the boat from cracking. The ritual protection came from natural substances collected on the territory such as fine clay, red powdery fungus that grows of the bark of the ceremonial cedar tree gathered in swampy places, and sap squeezed from the bark of particular cedars and said to be the trees' monthly flow — thus designating the tree as a feminine person and demonstrating the same potency also ascribed to the human female menstrual cycle among coastal tribes. The ingredients were gathered only from places on the family's territory that were perceived to be of special significance in that they are exposed to the sun's first light. The emphasis on the territory, as reflected in a symbolic *poiesis*, speaks to the experiential presence of people within a territory and the territory within the people. The natural substances from the territory are the ritual expression of the timeless union of land and people — thus, they serve as a ritual protection at sea that brings people back safely to the land.

Depictions of Territory as Iconic *Poiesis*

For the Kwakwala speakers, described by Boas (1966b) and Goldman (1975) as the Kwakiutl (now referred to as the Kwakwakawakw), who are located on the northerly tip of Vancouver Island and on the adjacent mainland coast, the presence of the mask in ritual was representative of the essential form of a spirit being, who was depicted or incarnate in the wearer and who possessed both human and animal spirit potentials: "The animal form of the ancestor was recreated as a mask — the ancestral crest" (Goldman 1975: 25). The crest for the Kwakwakawakw was the interior form of the ancestor, who possessed dual qualities, both human and non-human — with properties as animal or some other non-human form. Crests move according to precise patterns of either patrilineal or matrilineal kinship and provide a poetic iconography of enfoldment between humans and the non-human world, as explained above for the Gitxan. Moreover, nodal points in an individual life cycle, in concert with the cycle of the seasons, trigger the primary circulation of emblematic properties such as masks, names and songs, as if in a meshing of the gears between human cycles and natural cycles. Such a cyclical movement of property seems to occur in response to an involvement of Indigenous selves transcended towards their world. Thus, the cyclical movement of property becomes an expression of the vital forces, both natural and cosmological, that move in harmony with crests, powers and names, which represent still another set of vital forces, of status, rank and identity at the level of the social:

> We may start with the nature of emblems and their complements. The emblems represent an order of ancestral and mythological beings who achieve an incarnation within contemporary person. Through human beings, these beings are themselves transformed, as they in turn transform their hosts. The complements represent still other orders of life. (Goldman 1975: 126)

According to Boas, an animal skin is also a form of apparel, which transforms human inner properties into animal properties: "In myth, animals easily slip in and out of their skins to become momentarily non-animal" (Boas 1935b: 133, in Goldman 1975: 125). Throughout this work, we see the evidence of being-in-the-world as a shared process, between the human and natural world, in a mutual spirit of honouring and in an economy of reciprocity and sharing. Thus, the surrounding non-human persons receive valorization as spirit-beings and possess supernatural personhood. In mythological terms, the animal skin is seen as the animal's outer garment, by which the animal spirit — its power — can become separated from its body. Animal skins are thus similar in nature to masks: they embody and convey and impart the actual animal properties to the wearer through a ritual transmission. Within the context of Kwakwakawakw belief, animal skins are analogous to the animal spirits, as they are valorized in myths and form the material expressions of a folkloric *poetics* of involvement between humans and non-humans. Animal skins (unlike crests) circulate or are redistributed at a feast in response to the transmission of emblematic property, such as names and crests, which are conferred upon high ranking individuals at each stage of the life cycle, in concert with changes of the seasonal cycle. They are reminiscent of the drama of humans and non-humans within the nexus of a shared world — and the extended epidermal integument of the body-world synthesis. The animal skins become the extended or interchangeable skin of the human world as felt. They are the skins of an extended body, experienced as an enfoldment with the territory:

74

> In one myth, the hunter who has obtained the white mountain-goat skin has the power to catch other mountain goats. Thus the animal skin, *naenxwa*, which Hunt translates as "animal skin covering," and Boas renders more blandly as "blanket," is like a mask. (Goldman 1975: 25)

The discussion of the folkloric *poiesis*, as typifies coastal First Nations, gives testimony to a non-Cartesian experience of self's identification with the territory as it becomes expressive within environmental storyscapes.

Notes

1. The term "sacred landscape" has been borrowed from the field of cultural geography to describe a territorial region that was given to the resident people by the Creator (or another deity as is related within their ancestral folklore). It also incorporates sacred interpretations of landmarks and other features of the landscape. (See Stoffle, Halmo and Austin 1995.)
2. This section on alternating figures within a background explains how the repositioning of the body within a terrestrial background can alter its point of view on a given landmark or landscape, thereby changing the scene. Thus the body is shown to be the theme through which any background or landscape takes form and shape.

Chapter 5

The *Poiesis* of Land
in Interior Storyscapes

The Lower Thompson people believe the Dipper to be the transformers, the children of the black bear turned into stars. The Milky Way is called "the trail of the stars," or "what has been emptied on the trail of the stars." It is also called "the gray trail," or "the tracks of the dead."

> The Rainbow is said to have once been a man, a friend of the Thunder, who was in the habit of frequently painting his face with bright colors. (Teit 1900: 342)

The interior peoples of British Columbia share a similar folkloric transformer tradition to the coastal Stó:lō, which was discussed in the last chapter. The interior habitat of the southwestern plateau region, which is the homeland to the Salishan-speaking tribes, such as the Nlaka'pamux, Stl'atl'imx' and Secwepemc, is not a coastal climate; it is extremely hot in summer, arid and rugged. It is rocky in the extreme and jewelled with many salmon-filled lakes and rivers: it is mountainous, peopled with dramatic rock mortars thrusting out of the landscape and is frequently rent apart by deep, precipitous mountain gorges. It is in this formidable habitat that the people of the southwestern plateau have made their living for generations: within watersheds, harvesting mushrooms, digging roots, foraging for wild berries and other medicinal plants in the mountain valleys, and hunting mountain goat, alpine sheep and deer (Hill-Tout 1978a; Teit 1900; Turner, Thompson and York 1990). The Nlaka'pamux made their livelihood as if meshed with the land in a continuous and unbroken web of human and non-human phenomenon. The Indigenous people of this region live contiguous to the land, making their living in the watersheds of the Fraser, Thompson, Nicola and other surrounding rivers that demarcate their tribal territories. For the Nlaka'pamux, Stl'atl'imx' and Secwepemc people, as with the other tribal groups, the meaning of the land is passed on from generation to generation through the oral traditions carried by the elders, spiritual leaders and story tellers.[1] It is by way of these folktales, legends and myths that the meaning and dimensions of a territory is mapped out, described and understood; hereby the land is given historic content, significance and cultural dimension as the particularized, designated world of a specific people. In all cases the mythology, as given in the ethnographic record and oral tradition, ascribes a meaning to land which is both personal and sacred. Moreover, it is a reflection of the age-old, physical life activities of the people in particular families and communities within a geographic region. Each site of mythological significance represents the self-identification with the tribal territory of the Nlaka'pamux, Stl'atl'imx' and Secwepemc. These three tribes, which share a common body of similar and related folklore, also have age-old patterns of territorial use and creation stories similar to those of the Stó:lō sites Xeyxelemos and Mt. Cheam.

Each unusual rock or prominent mountain tells a story and orientates the people thematically in relationship to the territory. They map the land topographically on the basis of significant use sites, such as resting spots, territorial markers, fishing pools held by certain families, hunting areas, sites of worship, berry picking patches, etc. Thus, these prominent, iconically defined, mountains or unusually shaped landmarks anchor meaning on the land. They anchor the folklore and act as amulets of significance that map the interconnected spaces of interior Salish dwelling — they present an iconic *poiesis* of connectedness between a people and their territory. Such sites are reminiscent of being-in-the-world. The sites and corresponding folklore recollect the age old encounters of body and world at a particular place — they are geological statements of the extended body. "Most of the rocks and boulders of remarkable shape are considered as transformed men or animals of the mythological period" (Teit 1909: 596). Each folktale underscores the permanence of this reality with a reflexive legitimating statement, such as "these may still be seen there standing," which offers the opportunity of finding them at any time as they fulfill their role as thematic landmarks or defining figures for the Aboriginal people within the territory. To this extent, they secure the plateau world and the self-identification of the people as an active possibility.[2] In many cases, the mythological landmarks are animate or have personhood in that they are perceived to be transformed pre-human ancestors of the people living within the region. The folkloric belief throughout plateau tribes is that, in many cases, their ancestors or forebears survive to the present in rock form for all to see. A similar custom was also observed in the examples from the coast Salish Stó:lō in the last chapter. The land, through this means, has been folklorically incorporated into the plateau Aboriginal field of self. It is a case of the land speaking out, as can be described as an iconic *poiesis* on the imbrication of the people and land — a process that occurs through their life-sustaining actions at particular sites within the territory.

Interior Salish storyscapes and landmarks have common thematic links with the coast Salish study above. Geographic landmarks are obvious throughout the plateau region[3] (if you know where to look), are viewed as sacred sites, have been passed down to the present through the folklore of the people and owe their existence to occurrences in mythological time, when the earth was being formed and before today's humans existed, as is the case for the Stó:lō. The Nlaka'pamux, Stl'atl'imx' and Secwepemc (as well as other interior tribes such as the Okanagan and the Similkameen) believe that this mythological era was populated with important supernatural entities, especially the transformers,[4] who were able to change themselves and other beings into all manner of things (animate and inanimate) and who are seen as responsible for the world's features as they exist today (e.g., the introduction of fish and animal life to an area and the creation of certain geographic landmarks and mystical locations). The stories of these supernaturals are epic in character. The transformers themselves (powerful, supernatural beings) are always embarked upon a mythological journey, always travelling across the land, defining the surroundings, changing people into stone or heavenly bodies, and generally bestowing life and meaning throughout the region and its landscape. These epic journeys, as depicted in the mythology, serve as the *poiesis* by which this region's peoples experience the world. It is the means by which the Nlaka'pamux people become geographically situated within their territory, in accordance with well recognized and oft-experienced patterns of use that underlie a Nlaka'pamux field of self.

These epic journeys serve as a *poiesis*, or storyscape, whereby the world of these particular peoples acquires definition as a recognizable field of belonging and the means by which a figure (a thematically recognizable landmark of some kind) may become situated within a background of site-specific activities that make a location meaningful. The journeys of the many transformers over the plateau region, however, not only mapped the land but also rendered the moral teachings of the people on the rock faces or unusually shaped stones of this area by creating a storied landmark. Lessons such as what happens to bad people are told in association with the transformed ancestors turned into stone. Many lessons of this moral variety are evident, such as what misfortune occurs if you don't avoid a woman engaged in her puberty rites (as demonstrated as in the Secwepemc Thleesa fable, told below), or what can happen to men if they allow themselves to be lured away by a woman's beauty (as shown in the Nlaka'pamux Nicola Lake *nxa7xa7'atksw* tale, recounted below). This tale instructs people on the ills that will befall murderers, such as the brother and his beautiful sister in this story. The teachings connected with many of the landmarks anchor the moral universe onto the physical universe. Thus, the society's instructions are invoked each time the site is passed, therefore providing a *poiesis* of reflexivity on the issue of "real dwelling." The rock mortars throughout the plateau region are the containers of experience and moral wisdom as it has ancestrally emerged through the people's heritage and dwelling within the territory. These sites become the earthly messengers on how to dwell within the parameters of the culture.

The travels of the transformer deities such as Coyote, the Qwa'qt qwal Brothers and the Old Man (or Great Chief) lead to cunning transformations of many significant and evil pre-human people and monsters, known throughout the plateau as *spek'tl*,[5] into stone as the mythological proof of a supernatural's arrival at a particular, usually well-recognized, oft-used, geographic location. The various mythic routes of the transformers, for example, are literally peopled with transformed sacred rock landmarks that enliven and animate the surroundings with a definite personality and give concrete expression to the original presence of the supernaturals in the territory. The area is thus charged with possibility and meaning, with a mythic and ancestral presence, and its own recognized significance. The transformer rocks and sacred places become the themes for whatever else took place there; they are the markers of possibility that contextualize self, body and world. Throughout the various supernatural and mythic performances of transformers, an ancient and inseparable identification or belongingness is expressed between the people and their surroundings within a regional landscape, as was also shown for the Yanyedi people of the Taku River in the previous chapter. These important, humanlike landmarks, as the sacred locations of the interior Salishan speakers, are the subject of frequent discussion, are the site of visits and pilgrimages, and are seen as an ageless testimony on the heritage of the people in their land. Each folktale underscores the permanence of this reality with a reflexive legitimating, such as "These may still be seen there standing," which opens the possibility of their existence as historic markers, and of transformer journeys being legitimated or proven.

It is important to note, therefore, that the mythic achievements of the transformers are directly related to the matter of human possibility and the nexus of human activity within a landscape, as has been discussed in the case of Sweetie's camp in Stó:lō territory. The transformer stones become living expressions of the territory, through an internally coherent, experientially arranged, geographical process of articulation. The rocks provide the definite anchors of the location and act as the poles of action that orientate the practical movements of the human figures within the territory, whether they are doing fishing, hunting, berry picking etc. Within the body of creation myths that define the region, the transformers are depicted as journeying over the land, defining it, creating landmarks and otherwise integrating and incorporating the landscape physically within the world. Present in the mythology is the Old Coyote who, according to mythological record, was sent by the Old Man (much akin to the Creator) to put the world to rights (Teit 1898: 4). There were also three brothers named Qoa'ql qal (Qwa' qt Qwal), who travelled all around the country, generally transforming things and working miracles, and yet another transformer, who did similarly, by the name of Kokwe'la. All the above transformers, as well as the Old Man or Great Chief, travelled over the country transforming *speta'kl* into stone.

Further articulations of landscape occurred when the Old Man, also known as Old One, was said to have created much of the surroundings in the plateau region and to have "led the different tribes into the countries which they now inhabit, and gave them the languages they were to speak" (Teit 1909: 596). The quotation from Teit speaks to the assignment of a specific, supernaturally ordained, geographically articulated landscape. Of the utmost significance is that "mountains and valleys were given their present form by a number of transformers who traveled through the world" (Teit 1898: 19), generally changing the lay of the land and poetically re-making the world's geophysical features. These supernatural presencings in particular locations or places are said to have refigured the geographic features into what they are today, thereby re-organizing them as aspects of the world for a geographically select Nation within a storyscape.

In all cases, the landmarks which are told about in the folktales "can still be seen today" and show the people's journeys over the land; it is the process through which the world becomes solidified within the oral tradition of the people. The emergence of the world within the oral tradition occurs within a process of the extended self's position within a storyscape. "Most of the rocks and boulders of remarkable shape are considered as transformed men or animals of the mythological period." The Stl'atl'imx' and Secwepemc (Shuswap), as well as the Nlaka'pamux (Thompson) and Okanagan, according to Teit, similarly believe there were a number of transformers "who traveled about and gave the world and its inhabitants their present shape" (Teit 1898: 274).

Throughout the literature and folklore of the three traditions, the mythological interest in travelling is repeatedly stressed. Folklore from all societal groups throughout what is now referred to by anthropologists as the plateau culture area emphasizes that Coyote was on the earth a long time and travelled all over it in order to pursue his work. The Old Man was said by the Stl'atl'imx' to have travelled over all the Lillooet country but few traditions exist to illustrate his doings. According to Teit's ethnographic work on the Stl'atl'imx', the sun and the moon were also men who made alternate travels over the land, perhaps carrying light across the world as they went. The Stl'atl'imx' believe there were several great transformers, the greatest of which, perhaps, was Coyote, who was sent to the world by the "Chief," or the "Old Man," to travel over it and put it to rights He had four helpers — Sun, Moon, Mu'ipem, and Skwia'xenamux ("arrow-arm person"). In the myths he makes all the transformations himself, his helpers assisting him very little. Other great transformers were the Atse' mal, who were four brothers, their sister, and the mink. They always traveled together, and entered the Lillooet country from Harrison Lake, after having traveled along the coast. They never penetrated the land of the Upper Lillooet, where the Coyote had been traveling about. Other transformers who traveled through the upper Lillooet country were Tsu'ntia, the offspring of the root of Peucedanum macrocarpum Nutt; and Qwoqtqwetl, four brothers who traveled through the country of the Fraser River band. (Teit 1898: 274)

In the Secwepemc (Shuswap) tradition, the Old One was said to have travelled rapidly over the country performing much more than either Coyote or the others, who preceded him, in a shorter time. The Old One was said to be the chief of the ancient world, who came to earth to finish the work of his protégé Coyote and the other transformers. He was the transformer responsible for the earth as it is today. He travelled unrecognized, sometimes in the form of an old man, but also able to change his appearance. The Old One changed the land significantly as he travelled, raising it in some places and flattening it in others. "Where it was too dry, he made lakes; and where there was too much water, he made it dry" (Teit 1909: 596). No one knows what became of him, as is the case with Coyote, who may now accompany him. Once his travels were done, he disappeared to the east. Although the Old One and Coyote are significant transformers throughout much of the plateau culture area, in Secwepemc territory other transformers' travels were also significant. Ca'wa or Sa'memp (who taught the world various arts), Kokwe'lahait and Lee'sa (who rid the world of the many evil beings who are said to have preyed on people) also travelled the earth making changes. Throughout all of the creation stories we see how activities are represented both geologically and poetically (or symbolically), demonstrating how the land speaks out as a testimony to human activity and to human spatiality as an extended field of the self.

The Lillooet River Storyscape

There is significant evidence that the journeying of the supernatural transformers designated the important landmarks of the regional landscape in order to indicate important areas of use and to cement the recognized areas of the interconnected tribal territories (where dwelling traditionally has taken place) within an oral tradition or storyscape. Like most North American tribes, the settlements of the British Columbia plateau are clustered on the borders of the lakes and rivers of their habitats, designating these as important sites in establishing territorial boundaries and areas of use. As we shall show, the rivers and lakes as features of a given watershed, as well as primary fishing, hunting and foraging territories, figure significantly in terms of the fabled locations under study. The fabled locations, which are discoverable within the plateau culture area, are similar in meaning to those given in the chapter on coastal poetics.

In the case of the Lillooet tribes (or Stl'atl'imx'), the borders of the lakes and rivers of their habitat and intensive areas of tribal use are peopled with numerous transformed rock beacons, said to have been made by supernatural beings, which cohere with a north/south clustering of Stl'atl'imx' villages. Figuring prominently in the mythology are the edges of Harrison Lake and the Lillooet River in the Lower Lillooet tribal region, and Lillooet, Anderson and Seaton Lakes (to the Fraser River) in the Upper Lillooet tribal region. This continuum of lakes and rivers, being more than two hundred miles long and flanked by rugged mountains to the east, is the exact territorial region articulated in the Lillooet transformation stories:

> The villages ... are more or less bunched into two groups: one on the upper waters which flow northeast and one on the lower which flow south. This break in the settlements corresponds to a natural topographical one. It is here that the watershed or divide is found, which causes the rivers and lakes to run in opposite directions. (Hill-Tout 1978b: 101)

An interesting illustration of the poetics of landscape with respect to activity is given in the depiction of the Harrison Lake and Lillooet River territory of the Lower Lillooet people, who are a dispersed group of Stl'atl'imx' speakers. Lower Lillooet tales feature the journeys of the transformers Atse'mal (three brothers) as central in establishing geographical features, locations, landmarks and tribal boundaries within the territorial region of the Lower Lillooet. The tribal myths are classic transformer tales which profile the exploits of the transformers in their travels over the land, creating landmarks and defining territory to signify their presence within a place, to prove their "being there," thus defining the landscape and mapping it out for a linguistically specific group of human inhabitants. Throughout the folkloric journeys and reputed magical transformations, the ancient deities, as well as the *spek'tl* and ancestors, become merged with the landscape at certain important sites. They become personally integrated with the territory at the various First Nations named places. The landmarks and place names become the poetic symbols of the ancestors' original journey and actions within the territory and thus become constitutive of the Stl'atl'imx' world.

The legend tells us: "The transformers came through Harrison Lake into the country of the Upper Lillooet people" (elder Charlie Mack, in Bouchard and Kennedy 1971: 2).

As has been argued above, the folkloric mentioning of various physical bodies such as lakes, rivers, mountains etc. is the very means by which the land and territory are defined. It also situates the important landmarks (transformer sites) within their physical surroundings, to record the transformers' routes and to generally mark out the significant routes and the regional areas of involvement for the Lower Lillooet people. In this manner, the epic folkloric journeys of the transformers serve to situate the Lillooet people within their territory and facilitate their meaningful orientation, geographically. A figure must always be given meaningful definition against a background.

As the transformers (Atse'mal) were travelling in a canoe, which was their transformed sister, and heading along the Lillooet River (a primary settlement area for Lower Stl'atl'imx') towards a place called Lemp (a habitation site), they met up with Mink, whom they desired to turn into a rock. However, Mink was as powerful as they were, so they were unable to transform him. So instead, they invited him to accompany them on their travels for a time. Mink, who knew they were using their sister for a canoe, decided to sit in the canoe end and steer. He then intentionally caused the canoe to run aground near Lemp, where it smashed into a rock and left an imprint. The location is now marked for all to identify. "The imprint of that rock is still there today."

In the next sequence of the same tale (elder Charlie Mack, in Bouchard and Kennedy 1971: 2), we once again find depictions of the surrounding world that integrate a landmark with a territorial place: "Mink and the transformers continue traveling up the lake until they reached the mouth of the Lillooet River. Carrying on up the river, they came to a place that is called Shi-La-Posh, a very important fishing spot, where the shore is very rocky." Here, one of the transformers addresses Mink: "Mink, I think that we should leave part of your body here, because you are weighing down the canoe too much." Then they remove part of Mink's body and toss it on to the shore, where they transform it into a rock. "This rock can still be seen today"; this is a well-known fishing spot for the Douglas people.

After having done this, the transformers travelled up the Lillooet River and on into Lillooet Lake, where it is said that a great earthquake and flood once altered the rivers and lakes. Stopping at a traditional habitation site called Thla-lakwa[6] (near Mount Currie), they examined the marks that were left on the mountain's face from the receding waters of the great flood. The transformers then made each striped mark a different colour, and this mountain now is referred to as Shmi-mich, which means "marked mountain."

The oral tradition of the Lower Lillooet people (as related in Charlie Mack's narrative of "The Transformer") records hunting grounds, fishing grounds and viable passages through to the coast, as well as important territorial boundaries with the Squamish people, through a system of carefully articulated beacons or natural landmarks. Such geographic beacons serve as mnemonic anchors that contextualize the people within a storyscape that speaks to their being-in-the-world as an environmental reality within a particular site. Such contextualization can be observed throughout the Lower Lillooet's folkloric accounts. For example, upon pushing through the Lower Lillooet territory further, the transformers arrived at Zee-Hal-Im, where they discovered two men half way up the mountain called Ti-Zeel (a traditional hunting ground). At first they felt it was wrong to transform the innocent men into stone, since these men were only hunters. However, "The transformer wanted very much to transform them, so he changed them into the rocks which can still be seen today" (elder Charlie Mack, in Bouchard and Kennedy 1971: #2).

The narrative instructs us that the transformers passed next through Yi-Whi-La, a traditional Lower Lillooet fishing ground up the Birkenhead River, where they created a kingfisher haven. Near Birkenhead, at the summit, they took a rest and decided to leave proof of their presence at that place. "'We should leave a sign that we have been here,' said one of the transformers." They tried and tried, without success, to make a creek down the mountain. They then asked their sister to have a try, and, promptly, a white creek flowed down the mountain, where it can still be found.

After many exploits, and after going almost as far as the lower end of Seaton Lake, towards the modern town of Lillooet, they returned through Lower Lillooet country, heading back toward the coast by a different route. On their journey, they stopped at a place called Stsats-kwim, near Six Mile Creek, where the Squamish people were camping, and made some territorial landmarks to demonstrate the precincts of the Lillooet tribe, which indicated the outer reaches of their dwelling. "You are living very close to the Pemberton people, yet you speak a different Language. That is not right!" — the transformers told the Squamish people. "We are going to transform you into rock so that the coming people will know that we passed through this way." A large pile of rocks can be seen where the Squamish people were camped.

The tale details the route of the transformers on to the coast. They came to a place called Skeech-ik-thl-tin, near Alta Lake, and went along the Cheakamus River to a place called Skwee-Cho, where they transformed a chief who was living there into a rock. "This place is near the Cheakamus Power Station, and is in the territory of the Squamish people. I saw this rock, which is in the shape of a man, when I worked at the lumber camp. From there, the Transformers went through the Squamish territory towards the coast" (elder Charlie Mack, in Bouchard and Kennedy 1971: #2).

The Harrison Lake and Lillooet River region has traditionally been populated with habitation and village sites for the Lower Lillooet Stl'atl'imx' speakers, as shown in the archaeological record as far back as 1200 years ago (Stryd and Rousseau 1996, in Hudson 2000). The areas around each village were used for resource harvesting. Teit gives some information of resources and areas ownership (Teit 1906: 225–56). He says that fishing places in the area, and especially fishing weirs, were owned by families. The tribe (or group of people who were related) also owned in common other resource areas, such as hunting grounds, root-digging grounds and trails. Teit also says that berry-gathering areas near the villages were also family managed. Most of the resource use sites were concentrated on the Lillooet River (cited in the transformer stories above) and can be viewed as containers of meaning where social memory, human activity and folkloric depictions merge in what we have described as a storyscape.

Small specialized task groups or family groups frequently went on journeys around the territory, from the village sites to the hunting or gathering areas, either for day trips or for extended harvesting forays. Women went to gather berries and roots, while men went to hunt deer, mountain goats and elk. "Most of the resource use activities were and are focused on the Lillooet River Valley and a few key tributaries" (Hudson 2000). Extensive use patterns of hunting and gathering occurred in the highland areas within the Lillooet River drainage system. The coincidental nature of fishing sites and transformer sites is well known. These were obviously places where the oral traditions and the meaningfulness of the landscape were shaped. It is not surprising that the place where the A'tsemal lightened the canoe by tossing part of Mink's body out has been a celebrated fishing spot on the Lillooet River for many generations. Like Xeyxelemos in the former section, we see the animate nature of meaningful rock as a permanent and abiding marker or container for human dramas. The same profile can be seen throughout the Lower Lillooet territory.

In a version of Lillooet Stories edited by Bouchard and Kennedy (1977), there are several stories related to fisheries. A Mt. Currie story refers to a chief called In-CHEE-nim-kan (a name held by Baptiste Ritchie in the 1970s), who was said to control the salmon run "because he made the fish weir" (Bouchard and Kennedy 1977: 10). This story offers a lively depiction of a vortex of human and non-human involvement yielding waves of folkloric and poetic activity. The same body of information also contains a story relating to the large flood mentioned above, which was said to have swallowed all the low-lying ground in the region. To feed themselves during the flood, the people claim to have collected salmon roe. In one version of the flood-related transformer story (Bouchard and Kennedy 1977: 13–17), a salmon fishing place on Harrison Lake (STA-thli-lick) received a visit from the transformers that offer geological representation of the site's importance in depicting ancient human territorial involvement. Such stories anchor the Stl'atl'imx' people, historically, as being-in-the-world in the timeless sense.

Another transformer site is at Gates Lake, where the Lower Lillooet people say a small cleft in the rock is a footprint, which records the boundary between the Upper and Lower Lillooet territory (Kennedy and Bouchard 1977; Teit 1912). This marker lies at the top of the land amid two watersheds or drainage systems: to the west is the territory of the Mt. Currie people, to the east is the territory of the N'Quat'qua. The mark was described by a Hudson's Bay Company member in his journal entry for May 21, 1846:

> May 21. Fine. Set out at 4:30 am. At 6 reached a height of land where there is a large isolated block of granite bearing an impression closely resembles that of a human foot. The Indians call it Footstone and have of course a marvellous tradition connected to it. (Anderson, May 21, 1846)

In 1931 the location was also described by Elliot:

> The Transformer, Whalaymath came from Lillooet toward Pemberton (some say from Pemberton toward Lillooet). There were four of them and their sister was with them. They came to Tsekalnal (Birken Lake) and they saw that the waters of it emptied toward the east into Anderson Lake and the Fraser. One of them mounted on a big rock that was there and he urinated down the mountain side over the cliffs into the valley near Tsekalnal, and he said, "This stream shall always flow between Pemberton (i.e., the west). It will mark the boundary between the Lillooet and the Setl people." This is Squahilt (Foot, so called because the transformers left footprints there)." (Elliot 1931:168)

The Upper Stl'atl'imx' Storyscape

The same pattern of identifying the landscape to contextualize people's activities within a storyscape pertains to the Upper Stl'atl'imx' as well. An Upper Lillooet transformer story entitled "The Animals and Birds Got Their Names" (partially a Coyote story) demonstrates how mythological journeys establish a relationship between certain transformed geographic landmarks and places of importance for the people. A chief's daughter was uninterested in the local men, and, due to Coyote's trickery, was seduced instead by the chief's dog, which turned into a man at night. In only a short while, the girl gave birth to four puppies which grew into dog-children with the capacity to turn into human children at night. In other words, they had magical powers, which indicates an enfoldment of the human and non-human world as an interconnected process. The woman, who did not want the children to turn back into dogs, ran out with boughs and beat their dog skins where they had left them behind at night. However, to make a long story short, only the three brothers kept the human form, while the little girl remained a dog, for she had not removed her skin (elder Francis Edward, in Bouchard and Kennedy 1971: 4). The three became transformers and travelled over the land, attempting to rid the world of all people-killing monsters and, in so doing, established many important landmarks in the landscape.

After the mother had said good-bye to her sons, she remembered that she hadn't told them where all the monsters were. She, therefore, ran until she saw someone walking under the cliff at Hat Creek Junction (a place on the way to Cache Creek, close to the border of Secwepemc country), where she kicked some boulders over the edge of a ravine that rolled down towards the people. The boys welled at her with the words: "Hey, it's us! We are your sons!" The woman spoke with her sons, and then they carried on towards Cache Creek, which was as far as they wanted to go. This is likely emphasized because Cache Creek is in Bonaparte (Shuswap), near the boundary of Stl'atl'imx' and Secwepemc territory and, so, out of bounds. The itinerant path of the three sons began north of Pavilion (in Upper Lillooet), where the chief's daughter originated and raised her children. They toured the Stl'atl'imx' territory, travelling to Cache Creek and then, seemingly, went back through the Upper Lillooet to the Fraser River to a location known as "three mile," a well-known stopping point along the river trail. Here, the boys noticed a great rock that had a smooth face, and they left their bodily imprints in it for all to see, thus defining the landscape.

> "Let's see how far we can stick our head into this rock," one of the boys suggested. The youngest boy tried to push his head into the rock, but he only made a small dent. Then the second boy tried. He stood back and then ran towards the rock, butting his head against it. He sunk in as far as his ears. When the eldest boy butted his head into the rock, he sunk in as far as his shoulders. This rock can still be seen today. (elder Francis Edward, in Bouchard and Kennedy 1971: 4)

Once the three brothers had been successful on several occasions in ridding the world of dangerous beings, they went on to pass judgment on a succession of female *spek'tl*, changing them to stone and, thus, marking their passage through the landscape at important sites. They travelled to nineteen mile, another important known stopping point on the Fraser River, where they discovered an evil woman sitting beside a river. She had her legs stretched across the water, which necessitated that people must walk on them. The woman tried to kill Thlee-sa, the youngest brother, but couldn't do so. "'Never again will you kill anyone!' said Thlee-sa. He commanded the woman to walk away, at which point he transformed her into a rock. "This rock, which has a hole in it, can still be seen today." Thlee-sa and his brothers, on heading toward Moran, a habitation site, came to a place where a young girl was pressing her body into a rock in order to hide from them. "When the young men passed by, the girl came out of the rock, leaving an imprint of her body in the rock." When they got to Big Bar, another location on the border with Secwepemc, the three brothers noticed a woman across the river dancing and singing. As they watched her, the young men started changing into stone but, even as they were transforming, they noticed that she also was changing into stone. Thlee-sa had passed judgment on the woman, as she did on him. "Today, you can still see Thlee-sa and his two brothers on one side of the river and the dancing woman on the other side" (elder Francis Edward, in Bouchard and Kennedy 1971: #4). Such transformations in the Nlaka'pamux lore represent important historical sites in a similar manner to the Statliumx cases above — they serve to map out the territory, provide markers for human activities and are anchors of the Nlaka'pamux extended self.

The Nlaka'pamux Storyscape

In the *Nlaka'pamux* version of the tale, three Qoq'ql qual brothers came up from the S'a'tcinko country, at the Fraser River's mouth, and travelled through Lillooet country, continuously identifying the landscape as they went. After entering Nlaka'pamux territory from below, they followed the Thompson River and went on through the Bonaparte, Similkameen and Nicola valleys. Upon returning, went up the Bonaparte River and Hat Creek, planning to arrive back at the Fraser. "They did many wonderful things along the Fraser River changing people into fishes and also into stones. They also left their footprints and other signs in many places where they traveled and, it is said, created all the water springs over the country" (Teit 1898: 42). After encountering the great transformer Kokwe'la and also the Coyote people, they met a great man-eating magician named Tcu'isqa'lemux. He was spearing salmon on a bank at a fishing place named Zixazix, which means slides or mud-slide. It is on the south side of the Thompson River, in Nlaka'pamux country, four miles below Spences Bridge. The youngest and most powerful brother turned himself into a salmon in order to carry away the man's spearhead. Once the spearhead was safely stolen, the magician went home much disturbed for having lost it. That evening, the Qua'qlqal brothers ate dinner with the man-eater at his home. However, they soon became angry with Tcui'sqa'lemux, who was greedy over the food. Later on, when they again saw him fishing at the bank (indicating a fishing spot), they kicked the mountain down upon him four times in a row, which caused the mud-slide or "slipping mountain," which is there today. However, when the dust cleared away, he was still standing there. "Then they took revenge by turning into stone his house and basket, which are to be seen there at the present day" (Teit 1898: 44).

After they had travelled considerably farther and after many more exploits and competitions over power, they came across Coyote, who was sweat-bathing. "They turned his sweat-house into stone.... They turned into stone the basket, and the stones used for heating the water, and also tried to metamorphose the Coyote and his wife, but were not able to do so, owing to the too powerful magic of these people." Although the brothers were compelled to take flight, they were able to transform body parts from both Coyote and Coyote's wife, "which may be seen at the present day, with the basket at a little distance." They avenged themselves against Coyote for making them flee by breaking up his fishing weir, which stretched across the Thompson River at the well-known fishing spot known as Tsale'qamux. "The remains of the weir are what form the bar across the river and the rapid at that place at the present day" (Teit 1898: 44).

Further on, close to the mouth of Hat Creek, the three brothers had a competition over physical strength. A very large rock barred their progress and they decided to lift it on their heads and put it off to the side a fair distance away. Although the two elder brothers failed, the youngest one lifted it for a time. However, in so doing, the stone slipped over the upper part of his head. Upon putting the stone in the appropriate place, he withdrew, but a large impression of his head and nose near the bridge "may be seen at the present day." They continued their journey towards the Fraser River and crossed over the mountain above a village site called Q'qwa'ilox. Just before they crossed the open prairie, they observed a young girl who, while breaking from her puberty training, approached them dancing and singing (as in the Lillooet folktale described above). Upon stopping to watch her, the magic of the girl transformed them all into stone, where they "may be seen standing there at the present day" as a marker to the ancientness of the Nlaka'pamux self and as a representation of the people in the land and the land in the people.

The territory is thus given definition by the presence of mythological landmarks at necessary places. It is no coincidence that "Lytton is the center of the Nlaka'pamux map of the world" in Thompson mythology, "because here Coyote's son, when returning from the sky, reached the earth" (Teit 1898: 4), marking this spot as mythologically prominent, although no rock is now apparent. An interesting and central depiction in the plateau storyscape that relates directly to the poetics of land and territory is the "Earth Stone" site near Lytton, claimed by the locals to be the Nlaka'pamux centre of the world. In the legends, this one site has the profile as the "Centre of the Earth Stone" or "Coyote's Landing Stone." This is the site where Coyote's son (Coyote is a key mythological figure in plateau folklore, as well as a transformer) is said to drop from the sky country and make a landing on earth. This site has been cited by Boas (1885), Dawson (1891), Jenness (1934/35), Hill-Tout (1978c), Mohs (1987), and Teit (1900). Teit writes:

> Lytton is the centre of the world, because here Coyote's son, when returning from the sky, reached the earth. (Teit 1900: 337)

"NLi'ksentem Young Coyote found himself on top of a large flat stone near what is now the town of Lytton ... some of the Nkamtci'nemux say that the space on which he rolled himself was turned into this stone to mark the spot, for the Spider said that the place where NLi'ksentem should first touch the ground would be the centre of the earth or of the Indian's country" (Teit 1898: 25, 104). "N-kik-sam-tam reached the earth at Tl-kam-cheen (Lytton), and the stone upon which he descended can still be seen" (Dawson 1891: 30, in Mohs 1987: 106). Thus the Nlaka'pamux people hold this stone to be sacred, while, at the present day, they keep it covered with earth in order that the whites may not see it (Teit 1898: 30). A Stó:lō person of mixed Nlaka'pamux and Stó:lō ancestry writes:

> Where Coyote came down, there was a stone. I never personally saw this stone but I was told about it by my mom. She told me that no one would ever find it. It was buried really well so whites wouldn't see it. There was a fear among Indians in Lytton that whites would order that the rock be destroyed or taken away if they knew it was so important. So the Indians buried it. Beliefs in such things were considered wrong by the priests. Coyote's Footprints were on the rock because he ran around it many times. I was told it was a large rock and very smooth and you could see his footprints on it. But even though they tried to protect it, it was uncovered and destroyed. I don't know how. I never knew exactly where it was. (EP in Spiritual Sites File, in Mohs 1987: 106–107)

In 1898 and at the request of James Teit, an elder Nlaka'pamux man called Inaukawilich created a drawing of the earth as it was represented in the traditional Nlaka'pamux worldview. The world as he drew it was nearly circular in shape, bisected by rivers, level in the centre where the people were living in lodges at the confluences of the rivers, and very mountainous and precipitous near the outer edge. Beyond these mountains, the land was encircled with lakes that were thought of as the "water mysteries" and were covered with mists and clouds most of the year. Lytton (or Kumsheen) is seen as being the centre of the earth, according to this map, as in the Coyote mythology cited above (Teit 1898: 30).

The folklore and legends of the Nlaka'pamux serve to inextricably situate the Nlaka'pamux people within their surroundings as a unique and culturally defined region and territory, and demonstrate a history that reflects continuous ecological and ritual practices related to the land. The corpus of legends under study is thus understandable in terms of a *poiesis*, storyscape and enfoldment of self, body and world. The process of defining (or mapping) the landscape, both ritually and ecologically, is further demonstrated in the following story;

> As the Transformer neared Uta'mqt (or Lillooet) country, he saw people catching salmon with their hands at the Tsaxali's canyon, on the opposite bank. With their hands, they suspended boys from high rocks so they could scoop up fish. The Transformer, feeling sorry for these people, starts scratching the rock in front of him with his fingernails and with each scratch a helpful idea enters the people's heads. On the first scratch they decided to make twine, on the second to make nets, and so on, until they had acquired the full knowledge of catching fish. Once the people learned how to fish in the proper manner, the Transformer showed them the best fishing places, "and the Indians have always used these fishing-places or stations since that time." (Teit 1912a: 227)

Each scratch is a representation of a nexus of territorial activity and is a good example of a body-world *poiesis*. Furthermore, "the scratches in the rock, which the Transformer made when teaching the people how to fish, *may be seen at the present day*."

Plateau Storyscape as Personality

We observe, then, how the journeys of supernatural beings make changes and recreate the landscape, leave landmarks as beacons at specific important places and, generally, confer a sense of meaning and identity to the landscape. The landmarks have become the containers of human activity and meaning at sites where the people's "dwelling" takes place, and thus, such sites have absorbed personality. The geophysical landscape has been animated with a human presence, thus (following Merleau-Ponty) the human skin has entwined with other surfaces as an unbroken epidermal layer of sensibility and presence. The phenomenological conceptualization of the world as a "ratio of the senses" provides an explanation for the personalization of the land as seen here. As a result of what we have termed enfoldment, the land acquires personhood. The rocks, mountains and rivers have a definite identity or personhood. Expanding on this point, it is documented that the people addressed each mountain peak by name, or made offerings to them. "Many rocks throughout the country are looked upon as metamorphosed animals or people, or parts of people" (Teit 1906: 274). The surroundings become charged with a sense of who went before, with the bodies of the early people of the region (the *spek'tl*) cast in stone and as the anchoring of the epic achievements of the supernaturals in the geological bedrock. A connection exists between the physiognomy of the land and the characteristics of its human people. For example, near a location by the name of SLaha'l or SLaka'l, one can observe a man, a man's face with a twisted mouth and also a woman's privates. According to the Nlaka'pamux or Thompson mythology, upon introducing salmon to the Okanagan country, Coyote asked Wolverine for his daughter's hand in marriage. Once this request was granted, and once she brought forth a child, he threw her into the Upper Columbia River, where she lay down on her back and was changed into stone. "This rock forms part of the Falls of the Columbia, and the salmon ascend the river on either side of it." The folklore of the plateau region is peopled with such bodies.

Another good example of such personhood is found in the Lillooet's transformers. As the story continues, the transformers asked Tsoop (a fisherman) what he intended to do next, and he replied that he was making snowshoes in order to race the transformers, who were coming to his land. Upon discovering this, one transformer raced Tsoop down to his house. Tsoop made giant steps because he was in snowshoes, and so the transformer was dragging behind. Finally, the Transformer reached Tsoop's house and turned him into a rock. "But his eyes continued to blink," and "taking some paint, the Transformer's sister, painted in the eyes … which stopped him from blinking. This rock with the red paint on it can still be seen today" (elder Charlie Mack, in Bouchard and Kennedy 1971: #2). This demonstrates the integral relationship between humanness and land as a personalised field. In effect, eyes would seem to suggest the property of awareness, conferred for all time upon the aroundness of the landscape.

The indication of bodily impressions left in the stone by mythic characters is compelling evidence in demonstrating the interpenetration of the consciousness of the people with their surrounding landscape. Among the traditions of the Thompson River, for example, there was a transformer by the name of Kokwela, who originated from the root *kokwela*, and who travelled around the country changing bad people and those who offended him into stone. When he met up with the Qoa qlqal brothers, who were on their way up the Thompson River, he vied with them for magical dominance and vanquished them easily. Afterwards, however, they all camped together and now that spot can be readily identified by the bodily imprints left at their sleeping places. In the Lillooet transformer tale of Thlee-sa, a girl who was encountered near Moran in Stl'atl'imx' territory leaves an impression of her body while emerging from a rock hiding spot when the transformers were passing by. Imprinting such as this is also seen in the Nlaka'pamux transformer tale, when the transformer arrives near a location a few miles above Yale, known as E'am, where he meets a man of great size whose feet sink down into the rock as he walked. "He changed him into a stone, which may be seen a little east of that place. This man's footprints … may be seen at the present" (Teit 1912b: 228). Thus is personhood bestowed on the landscape with a visual tactile sign of the people in the land and the land in the people.

Recall at three mile on the Fraser River that the oldest Qoa qlqal (in the Thompson tale discussed above) sank his head and his shoulders into a smooth rock surface and that the impressions can still be seen today. In a parallel Shuswap tale, Tlee'sa and his brothers, who are engaged in their heroic journey to rid the world of man-eating monsters, decided to amuse themselves at a place near the mouth of Hat Creek called

> Little-coming-out-place (Puptpu'tlemten), where they saw smooth rock. Tlee'sa said "let's amuse ourselves by seeing who can stick his head farthest into the rock." The three brothers, one after another, pressed their heads against the rock, but made only slight impressions. Then Tlee'sa pressed his head against the rock, and it went in to the ears and bridge of the nose. When he pulled his head out again, a red mark was left in the cavity. (Teit 1909: 649)

It is almost as though he had been merged in union with the land for a time, where a real blood exchange had taken place.

In the Thompson River version detailed above, the Qoa'ql qal brothers finish their journey towards the Fraser River. When they cross over Mount S'qwa'ilox at Pavilion Creek (the location of the Shuswap village of S'qwa'ilox; the mountain, according to Teit, is very flat near the top, and therefore is called Spa'lEm by the regional people), they saw a young girl, who approached them dancing and singing and who turned them into stone as they stopped to watch her. *"They may be seen standing there at the present day"* (Teit 1898: 45, italics added). In the similar Shuswap version, "Kwelaa'llst has been sent out in haste to overtake the brothers and tell them of the mysterious power of Pubescent-Girl, and how to overcome her" (Teit 1909: 646). The brothers refuse to listen, and attempt to kill him by covering him with a slide of boulders, but he remained unharmed. Later in this tale, when the brothers encountered the Chipmunk near Hat Creek, who was also a pubescent girl, "She was dancing and they stopped to look at her. The brothers tried to transform her, but could not manage it properly" (651). At this point, the girl transformed them where they stood. "The Chipmunk girl became changed into stone of a red color, for she was painted red at the time; and the stripes, like those on a chipmunk, may still be seen on her back" (651).

The two references to red rock markings in this tale are interesting because they hint at the presence of painted human flesh and blood imbedded in the rocks — that the flesh and blood of the people is hereby commingled, permanently, with the ancientness of that land. In the Lee'sa tale, of the North Thompson people, a similar Tlee'sa incident is garnered, in which the breath of the supernatural and human realm commingles and the pigment of their red painted bodies become imprinted in the stones, showing the basic imbrication of mythic, human and natural worlds as geographic personality.

> The brothers came to a place on the North Thompson above the Red Trees Reserve, where, on looking over a cliff, they saw two Goat girls bathing in the river below. They had their bodies painted red. Lee'sa drew away their breaths by drawing in his own, and they became transformed into two red stones, which may be seen there at the present day. There is a cliff at this place near the river with a rock-slide at the bottom. (Teit 1909)

The folk tales abound with many more examples of transformed people in rock mortars throughout the land. In the Thompson tradition at a location called Huxtsi'xama, the transformer arrived at a place where a woman was in the process of birthing a child. The supernatural turned toward her and transformed her into stone. The transformer then went to Zolpi'px ("little *leha'l*"), where he changed all the gamblers into stone. "One man, who had gambled away his dog, was in the act of holding his gambling-bone behind his back and had his face turned towards his two wives, who were sitting nearby when the transformer turned them all into stone" (Teit 1912b: 228). A little *Secwepemc* story called "The War of the Four Tribes or of the Four Quarters" depicts, yet again, how landmarks were created from people. At a point in ancient times, the Cree to the east, the Nlaka'pamux to the south, and the Lillooet (Stl'atl'imx') to the west decided to attack the Shuswap (Secwepemc), who resided in the north. They all joined forces on the east bank of the Fraser River. Numbering several hundred, they advanced up river to attack the Shuswap but, when almost opposite the mouth of Lone Cabin Creek (still far from Canoe Creek), they met up with Coyote (or perhaps some other transformer), who transformed them into pillars of clay, and rendered these contiguous tribes into stone. These markers reference the actual tribal geographic regions that the respective tribes inhabit and demonstrate the presence of the people in the land and the land in the people. "They may be seen standing there now — the tall Cree on the right, the Thompson of medium height in the centre, and the short Lillooet on the left" (Teit 1909: 642).

Landmark *Poiesis* as Geographic Centres of Force

The landmarks created by the "heroic" supernaturals that travelled the world possess a definite ritual significance. These are the points upon which the world is anchored and thus are extremely important in the double-edged drama of human and non-human existence. As a result of their role in the disposition of human dwelling, they often have human names or resemble humans in some way and, therefore, are culturally and ritually empowered, while characterizing a living regional personality. The mythic landmarks in the transformer tales anchor and focus the oral explanations within a geographically articulated region. Thus, they are very compelling in mythological and ritualistic terms. In other words, they become the geographic centres of force, or centres of gravity, that Merleau-Ponty talks about in the *Phenomenology of Perception* (1962). These nodal points serve to ground the world in terms of the "possibility" of humans. As such, they become the anchors for the moral universe. However, the moral significance is not meaningful in the abstract, only in terms of what actually happened or happens there. The sites are the containers of human activity with its full spectrum of tones and meanings, which present the specific meaning and character of that place; they are the seats of Indigenous wisdom.

The Great Chief, or Old Man, or Great Man (all the same person) and the other transformer deities travelled over the country transforming bad people to stone, raising and flattening the land, making lakes and mountains and, otherwise, creating areas of use: hunting grounds, fishing grounds and significant landmarks as *sacred locations*. Consequently, certain mysterious powers preside in the topographical contours of the land. They resonate with the imbrication of humans and landscape in ritual or folkloric terms. They become animate, a quality that is reflected directly in the folklore, in what appears as supernatural qualities. Certain mountain peaks are seen as possessing land mysteries, and certain lakes are seen as possessing water mysteries. Other parts of high mountains, hills and other well-known landmarks can also be evoked through prayer or human invocation. For example, humans treading on given locations can cause it to rain or snow. In other places, it would only rain or snow when a stranger stepped on them for the first time (Teit 1900: 344).

> The land mysteries live chiefly in mountain-peaks and caves; and the water mysteries, in certain lakes (especially those having no outlets), and in waterfalls, bogs, and springs in the forest, particularly those surrounded by moss and reeds. (Teit 1909: 598)

Many of the mountains in the plateau region are said to have such sacred power. Water mysteries (known as Transformer locations in the form of men, women, grisly-bears, fish and so on) are said to emerge from the water, the sight of which is fatal to any onlooking man, woman or child. The lakes and mountains in the Cascades have water mysteries, and the high mountains to the west and south of Lytton have land mysteries. These important areas in the landscape have a unique supernatural personality; they represent a mysterious power. There is a lake between the three mountains, near Foster's Bar, in which strange mysteries may be seen (Teit 1900: 338).

One place of this kind is on the west side of Fraser River, opposite Fosters Bar, in the country of the Upper Fraser band. There are three high mountains here — the highest one, in the middle, is called A'motEn and is believed to be a man; his wives are on each side, called Ntekelxtin and Se'ijuk. If an Indian at any time takes a stick, and threatens to strike, or makes the motion of striking A'moten with it, it will at once rain. The Mountain Kazik, near Lytton, was also believed to possess supernatural power. When a person who had a strong guardian spirit pointed at it, it would rain. Still another mountain of this kind is the peak Skoia'iks, north of Spences Bridge.

Mountains in Nlaka'pamux territory were seen to possess a particular and very potent ritual power, integrally connected both to the human and animal worlds but also to the cosmic world. It was the contours of the earth that manifested and appeared, folklorically, through supernatural miracles as explained above. When an Nlaka'pamux mother went root digging at the site of a sacred mountain with her baby for the first time, she would paint her entire face red, and sometimes the top of her head. Afterwards, she would dance before her infant, perhaps for the whole night, praying constantly to the spirits of the place or to the mountains themselves "asking that her child might never be sick, and that, if it were ever bewitched, and no shaman were near to help, nevertheless it might not die, or that she herself might have power to defeat the evil" (Teit 1900: 309). Kneeling down, spitting into her hands and rubbing the body upward, over the face and over and down the back of the head, she prayed that she might be delivered from all disease or trouble, that she would never be bewitched or hurt and that, if ill, she would recover soon. At Po'pEsamen, which means "Little Heart" and is located on Upper Bridge River in Stl'atl'imx' territory, the people who went to hunt and camp in the area visited a "certain place" at the top of the peak. Once there, they addressed the mountain, saying "O Chief! Don't rain or fog. Give us easy root-digging and successful hunting. Take all smell from us, so that the game may not scent us!" (Tait 1900: 309). These sacred locations and landmarks emerge as particular charged sites within a mythologically defined, geographically articulated world, where human and non-human agents share a common enfoldment.

The women, when picking berries or digging for roots on certain mountains that were defined as sacred, would always paint their faces red.

They also do this before coming upon sacred lakes, in order to be favoured with good hunting and good fishing. When they approach a sacred location, they offer up a blessing or a gesture of good will to the spirit of the place, to bring good weather and good hunting (Teit 1900: 344). "These offerings generally consisted of a lock of hair, a rag from the clothing, a little powder, a few shot, a piece of tobacco, a stone, and so on" (344). Paint also was used as an offering.

Another sacred location, recorded in Nlaka'pamux lore, is Nicola Lake. Evidently, in early times, a man named Stemalst lived there with his sister, a mountain goat, who was a beautiful female. As the story goes, whenever anyone travels along, especially men, this beautiful woman lures them into the house, now called nxa7xa7'atkwa, which translates to mean "the sacred waters of Nicola Lake." "She would invite them in for something to eat and her brother would kill them and eat them. The whole outside was a pile of bones" (Hanna and Henry 1996: 79).

When the transformers came up from the coast, they concerned themselves with these goings on. The youngest of the four brothers, wishing to test his powers before returning home, went on ahead of the others to be grabbed by Stemalst and, consequently, was invited by Stemalst's sister to partake in a meal. Afterwards, Stemalst killed and ate the young transformer and threw out the bones. In revenge, one of his older brothers transformed Stemalst and his sister into two stone mountains, "the sister, being on the south side and the brother being on the north side" (Hanna and Henry 1996: 79). We are told, also, that the lake was built between them, because Stemalst had been having intercourse with his sister. The lake, furthermore, is said to be the transformed dogs of Stemalst and his sister. Thus, the waters of Nicola Lake have always been sacred to the people of the area. If people desire strong powers of medicine, they go to the lake slowly, while praying to the mountains. It is inappropriate to bathe around these waters, and there still exists considerable fear of this place. "*Xa7xa7* is kind of a spooky, scary, unpredictable thing" (79). The people would also sleep on these mountains for power (Teit 1909: 596).

Another supernaturally created landmark documented as a sacred location is Xa'lil, near Fort Yale in Thompson country. Here, the people had several (four or more) large seats or blocks, shaped like trunks, on which they would sit. The Old Man turned these, plus a man of very large proportions, into stone, and "he may be seen at the present day lying on his back" (Teit 1912b: 228). This transformation site marks a mystical site for the Nlaka'pamux, as the people go to these stones whenever the weather is hot and rub on them, which is said to make the skies turn immediately cloudy. If it is rainy, they do the same thing and the sun comes out. This is a marked portrait in the *poiesis* on human and non-human enfoldment.

In the Upper and Lower Thompson myth of Qwa'qtqwetl and Kokwe'la, a similar legendary phenomenon can be found. In this story, the Qwa'qtqwetl brothers and Kokwe'la travelled together for a time, combining their powers. As they proceeded up the Thompson River, they met a young woman, some say an adolescent girl, who was a snake woman who ensnared men. She "called on all male passers-by and made love to them. When they succumbed to her enticement, her vagina closed, and severed or crushed their genital organs, and thus killed them." The brothers discovered the woman prone at the side of the trail with her legs spread open, which was her way. The youngest and most powerful of them decided to overcome her and separated her labia with his arrow flaker, which prevented her parts from closing on him. "'Henceforth no privates of women shall have the power to destroy men.' This rock is there yet." The transformed rock has a crack in it that resembles female genitalia and is a good example of how a transformed, human-like landmark could function as a sacred location and how the power ascribed to a particular mythological place likely stands testimony to the power and danger inhering in female puberty rites. The rock is viewed as mystical or powerful for the regional Native people, who go to the rock and pray for the healing of their swollen limbs. "They strike the rock and the affected parts of the body with fir-branches, asking the mystery of the place to cure them" (Boas 1969 [1917]: 17).

Another transformation of mystical significance occurred in this tale about a place now called "Gaping" or "Open Mouth," near Drynoch. The story tells how a giant horse living at this place caught people in its mouth. "People simply walked into its open mouth when it placed it on the trail. Qwa' qtqwetl, the transformer, placed his arrow flaker between the animal's jaws so they could not be closed, thus killing its power, and turned it into a stone which can be seen today, and the place is now recognized for its sacredness and mystery" (Boas 1969 [1917]: 17).

The further consecration of the landscape arrives through the fact that the deified transformers, such as Coyote, are bodily enshrined within the landscape at various places, representing a sacred meaning and special importance to specific locations. This is often seen in the transformation of significant body parts, indicative of the extended bodily surfaces of body and world referred to in Chapter 3. Frequently, sexual anatomical parts impart extra power onto the landscape: "There they also changed Coyote's penis into stone. It may be seen sticking out on the south edge of the mountain as an isolated peak" (Boas 1969 [1917]: 17). Such an iconic representation speaks to the acknowledged gravity of the relationship between people and land. In various cases, where the most visible landmarks are seen as a supernatural's private parts (as occurs quite frequently in the plateau region), a poetics of force speaks in iconic terms about the people in the land and the land in the people, in a relationship of indelible and titanic meaning.

Notes

1. Although the interior peoples of British Columbia are unlike the coastal peoples, in that they lack a unilineal system of descent (such as matrilineal or patrilineal) as seen, for example, in the Nisga'a and the Gitskan, they do demonstrate an inheritance structure pertaining to rights and territory based on the bilateral/kindred family system, in that both sides of the family figured significantly.

2. Active possibility refers to the ability of humans to situate themselves in meaningful space in order to participate in the world.

3. The term "plateau" refers to the "culture areas approach" of anthropology, which classifies First Nations within British Columbia in terms of primary cultural areas of like or similar cultures. The three areas are coastal, plateau and sub-arctic. The plateau is in the centre of the province on what is known as the Central Plain.

4. Transformers are folkloric figures, central to plateau creation stories, who came to earth prior to the habitation of humans for the purpose of putting the world straight and preparing it for habitation by humans.

5. *Spek'tl* is word that refers to pre-human ancestors that are characteristic of the interior Salish oral traditions across the central part of British Columbia (known by anthropologists as the plateau culture area). Such *spek'tl* were considered to be evil and dangerous to human habitation of the area. Thus much of the plateau folklore is devoted to epic stories about the vanquishing of the *spek'tl* by supernatural travellers known as transformers. The folkloric myths and stories from the area describe the large stone landmarks around the area to be the transformed bodies of the *spek'tl*.

6. "Thla-lakwa" shares a phonetic resemblance to "zazi-lkwa," meaning eddying waters. Recorded by Charles Hill-Tout in his account of the Stlataumh (Stl'atl'imx). See Hill-Tout 1978b: 103 and Hill-Tout 1978c: Pt. 5: 293.

Chapter 6

The *Poiesis* of Enfoldment within the Stein Valley Storyscape

> You wanted to be an Indian Doctor, if you want to be big chief or a powerful man you go to the creek and then you use that fir bough and you talk to the morning and to the creek. So as you'll talk to them — you ask them for guidance, so as you live a long time in this world and you wouldn't get old so quick, and you ask for their guidance to help you so as you become an Indian Doctor. Then you'll become a man — if you want. You'll go to the big mountain and you'll prepare yourself to become whatever you want to be. (Speech by Chief Tetlenitsa, 1912, in M'Gonigle and Wickwire 1988)

Paralleling the illustrations of the previous section, much of the surrounding landscape in the Stein Valley, a valley sacred to the Nlaka'pamux and also to some extent to the Stl'atl'imx' people, has poetic, mythic and ritual significance and also a "narrative meaning" within the legends and tails of the Nlaka'pamux and Stl'atl'imx' people. The Stein Valley has been declared the Nlaka'pamux Stein Tribal Heritage Park under the B.C. Ministry of Parks and Recreation and is co-managed with the Nlaka'pamux First Nation. The sacred value of the Stein has been established as a result of the many age-old Nlaka'pamux stories and traditions that have evolved there and the corresponding symbolic sites, such as landmarks, rock paintings and place names. A key heritage feature of the Stein River area is vested in the trail moving along the side of the Stein River, which for generations has been the access path from the mouth of Stein Creek through the middle Stein and up to the higher altitudes. According to M'Gonigle and Wickwire, when writing of the Stein, there is "a rich complexity of life woven into a dynamic wholeness that pulsates with vitality, yet is quiet to behold. In the flow and dance of a running stream is the movement of life itself" (M'Gonigle and Wickwire 1988: 19). This is understandable in respect to the previously outlined theory of self, body and world. The trail beside the Stein River, with its many stories, becomes the poetic container for all that happened there within that centuries-old vortex of human and non-human activity. Worn with the weight of generations of foot traffic, this access trail has been the pathway of aspirants on spiritual quests, of women going into the middle Stein to pick oyster mushrooms (*kumash-ekwa*, at Shklimeen or "wade across place") and harvest cedar roots for baskets (at *kiskw* or *kemkamatshoots*) and of families migrating to a place near "canoe landing," or *shtli-heel shtlahkows*, to engage in night fishing, which is done with a pitch lamp shone into the dark waters to see the fish.

Late Nlaka'pamux elder Andrew Johnny described travelling ten miles

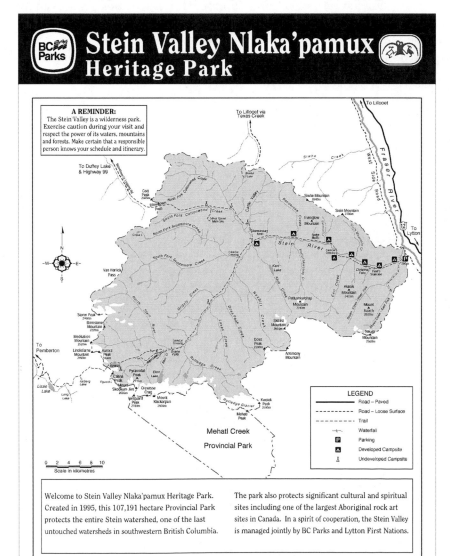

up into the Stein Valley in wintertime, when the snow was too deep to use the trail. In those conditions, Nlaka'pamux men used to travel on the frozen surface of the river to get into the valley, and they could look through the ice and see the fish below (*The Stein* 1988). This shows the cyclical, seasonal web of human and environmental activity. Special rituals are also associated with the Stein Valley. The rich combination of human practices, both economic and spiritual, typify what is meant by a regional landscape, as discussed in Chapter 3 (Stoffle, Halmo and Austin 1995). The landscape of the Stein region presents a corresponding storyscape that maps the land (in terms of human possibility) at various sites within this vast and complex organism of human and non-human activity which is the valley. The Stein Valley is full of ancient stories and mythological landmarks, still alive in the oral traditions of the Nlaka'pamux people and, thus, forming a regional *poiesis* of the Valley's activities. "The Stein cannot be appreciated fully except in this total way — as a wild river, complete watershed, place of spiritual power and root of native culture" (Wickwire 1988: 20).

The Stein as an Nlaka'pamux storyscape and regional landscape dovetails with the wider Nlaka'pamux folkloric depictions of transformers. The Sesuli'an and Seku'lia were part of the group of transformers known as the Shkwitkwatl, which came from Secwepemc country and reached Styne Creek (the Stein River). Teit's recollections follow:

> Two Transformers, Sesulia'n and Seku'lia, came down the Fraser River from the Shuswap country. They were good men, and taught the people many arts. They transformed those who were proud, while they helped those who were grateful for advice and instruction. They reached Styne Creek at dusk. A number of people were living in an underground lodge just north of the creek, and their dogs began to howl when the Transformers approached. A man went out to see who was coming. When he saw the Transformers, he made fun of them. Therefore they transformed him, the house, and the people into stone. When leaving this place, Sesulia'n left the mark of his right foot on a stone, and a little farther down the river Sekul'ia left the mark of his left foot. Both these impressions of human feet may still be seen in the woods near Styne. (Teit 1917: 13–14)

The Stein Valley's mythology also documents encounters with the "animal people" who reside in the valley's many recesses, where both spiritual empowerment and renewal are said to be gained. Coast Salish people claim that the spirit animals in the coastal region were vacating the woods, around and about, due to the growing prevalence of humans (Amoss 1978). However, the Stein wilderness still holds an intact spirituality in the eyes of the local elders. The body of folklore present indicates the non-dualistic kind of enfoldment of human and non-human agents discussed in Chapter 3. For example, Native people, such as the Nlaka'pamux of the British Columbia plateau region, embark on vision quests during both puberty rituals and shamanic training in search of a guardian spirit animal. The guardian spirit animals, called *sne7m* in the Nlaka'pamux language and attained at the time of the vision quest, are reputed to be found in the most remote reaches of the forest. This spirit acquisition is deemed possible because of the fact that nature is perceived to be imbued with spiritual power (Teit 1900: 354) similar to the kind discussed in case of the Gitxan. Continuing with this notion, the spirit power was said to be given to a young person by some non-human agent or animal (like the wind or water, bear or wildflower) and, henceforth, would become integral to their personal sense of self. This manifestation — or *sne7m* — would become the person's guardian spirit and source of personal power.

As Louis Philips, an Nlaka'pamux elder puts it, "Indians those days: there wasn't one Indian that hasn't got a certain amount of power. Soon as you big enough, go in the bush there and stay out there.... That's why they go up the Stein, maybe thirty miles" (Teit 1900: 35). He also explains "that nature, when you get enough power, gives you a song that you gotta sing for different things you gotta do." It is believed that the individual's spirit animal, during puberty rituals, provides the vision-questing youth with a song that stays with him or her throughout their lifetimes. This song serves as the vehicle that rouses the *sne7m* — or spirit power — for the individual's personal use. Such a sonic/iconic form of *poiesis,* expressing the experiential fusion of human and non-humans, finds a complementary form of expression in the Stein through other iconic/aesthetic visual art forms, which were employed to speak to this experiential fusion of human and non-humans, as seen in the many rock paintings. The rock pictures recorded the spot where a vision occurred and were usually in geographically dramatic or awe inspiring places of sound or view, where the natural agents seemed most powerful. Such an imbrication of body and world gives rise to the many historical representations that serve as an environing *poiesis* of self, body and world. Teit reports:

> Lads painted records which were pictures representing their ceremonies and their dreams, on boulders, or oftener on cliffs, especially in wild spots, like canyons, near waterfalls, etc. These were generally pictures of animals, birds, fishes, arrows, fir-branches, lakes, sun, thunder, etc., figures of some symbolized their future wives. It was believed the making of rock paintings insured long life. (Teit 1900: 321)

The untouched wildness of the Stein is said to be necessary for the survival of this spiritual heritage that is the Aboriginal birth right and tradition of both the Stl'atl'imx' and Nlaka'pamux people, who both use the Stein.

Many of the landmarks given below are at the mouth of the Stein, a habitation site for the Nlaka'pamux and a place of intensive human activity and involvement. Other areas further into the valley are also age-old harvesting sites (for mushrooms, cedar root, fish, etc.) and have vivid and literal depictions in sonic space through a large number of Aboriginal place names that tell exactly what goes on there. The oral traditions that contextualize the Stein landmarks and designated sites give testimony of an ancient heritage, while the self-identification of the Nlaka'pamux and Stl'atl'imx' people in this regional landscape provides a meaningful *poiesis* of dwelling within a territory of age-old tribal belonging.

Alongside the trail leading from the church to the main graveyard and to family fishing stations on the Fraser River, two child-size footprints can be found. The local people explained these as belonging to the *spek'tl,* the first ancestors, known to be half-human, half-animal, who occupied the world when it was new and are said to be the predecessors of humans. These two footprint-marked rocks are familiar to all who spent time at Stein Village up until the 1960s and seem to resonate with the human activity that takes place there. "You walked by them," as Louis Phillips explained, "at every funeral" (the one near the church is to the right of the foot-trail just behind the church, and the other is on the left side of the trail, just north of the main graveyard) (Wickwire in Elsey 1997). Another well-known landmark of cultural significance is a spring, from which water was obtained by the people of the Stein during wintertime. This spring (with the Native name of *skwel'altkwo,* which means "hole in the ground") was located a short distance northwest of the church (Wickwire in Elsey 1997). The spring area was modified to create a small pool for bathing after a sweat bath.

According to Ina Dick (of Stein Village) and also Louis Phillips, there is a large bedrock near the well-used trail, a short distance south and west of Stein Village on the way to Npat´us, the first small mountain ridge on the north bank of the Stein. On this rock, it is claimed that you can find the imprints of what looks like a deer and a bear. Louis, however, reports that the footprints are of a bear and a goat and were left there after the Great Flood, which was mentioned in a Lower Lillooet story (Wickwire in Elsey 1997). Thus they are an integral part of the place and have mythological significance. It seems they encapsulate an ethos of human activity dating back to a flood in ancient times and so are an important marker of belonging between these people and that land in the ancient sense.

According to Louis Phillips, as you look across to the Stein from the east bank just above the group homes (just north of St. George's farm) you are able to spot the outline of a woman lying in a prone position on the peak of Mkíp. She is referred to as "sleeping beauty" by the locals living at the mouth of the Stein and is seen as an important landmark and sacred site. Referring to the same mountain, Trit reports: "The Mountain Kazik, near Lytton was … believed to possess supernatural power" (1900: 345). Both Q'i'q'azik and Mkíp were known to be particularly powerful. Close to the mouth of Last Chance Creek is a large panel of pictographs.[1] It sits high on a rock face, and underneath it there is a ledge that is big enough to stand or sleep on. This place is clearly associated with spiritual power. Archaeologist Harlan Smith tells us that, in 1897, a local Native named Jimmie claimed this to be the place "where boys and girls came to wash with fir boughs" (Wickwire in Elsey 1997) and associated a great deal of importance with this place. The pictographs are representations of the synthesis of body and world, and of all that has gone on in this place. Charles Hill-Tout commented on pictographs:

> Certain spots and localities are pointed out by the older Indians as the places where certain celebrated shamans underwent their fasts and training to gain their powers. There were several such spots on the banks of Stein Creek.… Worn and hollowed places are pointed out here and there, and these are said to have been made by the feet of the aspirants after shamanistic powers in the performance of their exercises. We find several groups of rock paintings along this creek which are believed by the present Indians to have been made in the past by noted shamans. (Hill-Tout 1978a: 48)

There are three pictograph sites closer to Teaspoon Creek (a small creek in the lower Stein, which Andrew Johnny calls Sìsq'w). The first one is a cave-like structure where one has to lie down to view the paintings and which has special significance for the people. Also at Teaspoon Creek, a grove of culturally modified trees is found, demonstrating this region as a well-travelled part of the Stein. Culturally modified trees are cedar trees, the bark of which was formerly harvested for clothing, and they are seen these days as a meaningful cultural resource and landmark (Wickwire 1988: 27).

Located on the cliffs over the north bank of the river near "crossing place" is a deep cave that is painted with pictographs from top to bottom. The oral tradition maintains that some Native people were ice fishing west of Lytton on a lake, when they followed a goat up the cliffs to this cave and found it to be totally painted (M'Gonigle and Wickwire 1988: 49; Wickwire 1988: 31). The lake in question is likely the area above the cable crossing, described as "the place of still waters," because here the river is wide and the water is very calm. Thus, the place name speaks poetically of the river's state and characterizes body-world *poiesis*. The name of the place reflects the sensual impressions of the river as perceived by the lived body. It looks like a lake, and in the winter it freezes over and is considered a special place.

Underneath a boulder along the Stein River there is a special place signalled by a cave-like opening, under which the locals say Nlaka'pamux women used to give birth. After the baby was born it was brought down to the river and bathed in two circular pools eroded in the rock. Recently, fires were built in the pools, which purportedly have destroyed this sacred spot, and it is rumoured that the spirits have vacated it. However, it is still perceived to be deeply meaningful as a traditional spot of sacred geography, amplified by what was done there.

The same analysis applies inside the biggest painted pictograph panel, *Asking Rock*, a narrow ledge with two smooth, elongated stone hollows that are large enough for people to lie on uncomfortably while gazing at the pictographs. Elders, such as Willy Dick, recall a time when these natural stone beds were lined with spruce boughs, which are associated with puberty rites and are also known as birthing stones, where Nlaka'pamux women went to give birth. Later, the baby would be baptized in the waters of the Stein (Lepofsky in Elsey 1997: 11).

Stein Place Names in the *Poiesis* of Body and World

The study of place names in the Stein Valley speaks with particular poignancy to the poetics of self, body and world in a way similar to the rock art. It raises the question of what is embodied in a place name. To harken back to the discussion of phenomenology in Chapter 3, we can re-ask at this juncture the question of how does the land speak? The answer in phenomenological terms looks first to the human perception of places on the land and how this is depicted and inscribed within a living vocabulary that gives oral reference to significant places as they are passed down from generation to generation — thus, the land speaks! However, the land's speaking out is as much about human doings as it is about the non-human setting. The place names in the Stein, therefore, are testimony to human activity and goings on at a particular place. They connect to the particular sites of dwelling within a regional landscape, providing an oral map of the relationship between people and land. Place names, therefore, are better when they are precise in terms of the site they represent, for that way they present the clearest reference for territorial activities and territorial histories, these are passed down through generations. The place names thus, are an expression of not only how the land looks, smells, feels and sounds, but also of what happens there (e.g., mushrooms are harvested, a fish weir exists, cedar roots are gathered). These represent the vortex of human and non-human activity that is evident at that place, as Bierwert explains with respect to Sweetie's camp, mentioned in Chapter 4. Named places become a poetics of the body-world nexus and flow, similar to landmarks and painting sites and as thematized, topographical anchors for human activity belonging within a place. Human existence is given definition through such well-known places on the land, and dwelling can occur on an intergenerational basis on a foundation of prior experience — on this basis ancestral self-identification to place becomes a lived reality.

The Stein Valley place names are a good example of how Aboriginal place names provide a linguistic map of the territory and give a description of the land at a certain place, after the manner of the land's speaking, as explained above. For example, Kemkamatshootsi Umya means "small area where yellow avalanche lilies were found" (Chris Arnett and Angus Weller 1991, in B.C. Parks 1997). This place, which is vividly depicted in terms of topographical description but also in terms of what happens there, is also claimed by a Nlaka'pamux elder to be a spot where the people dug cedar roots for basket production. It has, furthermore, been explained, that Kemkamatshootsi Umya likely also refers to a large grove of culturally modified trees (harvested Aboriginally for their cedar bark) a mile north of Tsikwoxowks, a creek on the north bank of the Stein River, across from Tsiwetetem. Tsikwoxowks, a mountain in the area, is the Nlaka'pamux word for "red-headed woodpecker," according to Nlaka'pamux elder Willie Justice and is applied to the creek that flows down it also. This same creek is also known as Battle Creek, recalling an ancient skirmish between the Stl'atl'imx' and Nlaka'pamux. Tsikwatete is the Nlaka'pamux word that means "red inside" and is given to this area because of the unique red colour of the rock face on the south side of the river. This site is traditionally known by the Nlaka'pamux people as a gathering place to collect sacks full of *Katsha* or Labrador Tea. A mineral spring, where the animals go to drink, is also said to be situated nearby. Upon analyzing the three related named places above (Kemkamatshootsi Umya, Tsikwozowks and Tsikwatetem), we see an imbrication between humans and geography where the land speaks, providing vivid oral articulations to sonic space of what can be seen there or felt there and, also, on the nexus of human doings at that site. It is as if an interconnected flowing and moving together of people and land vividly marks out the dimensions of the territory and is welded into oral memory through the ancestral repetition of the place names — the land speaks!

Nukwanukwits, the Nlaka'pamux word meaning "cottonwood creek," is actually called Cottonwood Creek in English. The oral tradition has it that an Indian doctor built a sweathouse close to the mouth and beside a waterfall. These memories are now incorporated in the depiction of the place name. According to the Nlaka'pamux, the waterfall there is associated with the water mysteries attributable to a creation story of the Nlaka'pamux. The cottonwood drainage is a traditional hunting ground, used in ancient times up until the present. The Nlaka'pamux elders claim that the "old Indians" hunted for mule, deer and mountain goat in ancient times, "way up at cottonwood." These animals are still to be found there in wintertime.

Another good example of the extended embodied flowing together of people and land, as it is contained within a named place, is found in the name Skeetaytn. The exact location of Skeetaytn is uncertain, although it is claimed generally to be between the cable car crossing (*shklimeen*) and Nukwanukwits. The name Skeetaytn means in Nlaka'pamux to "get up on top." It is believed that this name refers to a segment of the trail that climbs up and over a rock outcropping in order to avoid a marshy area. This nicely depicts the poetics of body and world, and the manner in which a body can be thought of as a locality or as a bodily opening outwards onto the world, in a way that demonstrates how experiences can be inscribed in a body-world poetics. A similar example of body-world poetics is found in the place name May-humtm. It refers to a place in the Stein where the Aboriginal people harvested cedar roots for baskets and literally means "infested with bugs," thus speaking to the nexus of human and non-human activity as it is voiced as a living reality of what is there.

Nukwqanukwits utsiyem, literally meaning "small area where cotton-wood is found," is an exact description of the place in human terms. It is a traditional place used by the Nlaka'pamux to dig cedar roots for basketry. Another example of body-world *poiesis* (as it is articulated in place names) is Shklimeen, which means "wade-across place" and recalls a bodily locale: the place where the Stein trail crosses over the river from the south to the north side over a shallow gravel bar. This named place, which is indicated by a large painted boulder, is a container for numerous traditional activities, which provide it with its lived significance. Nlaka'pamux women made camp at this place in order to dig cedar roots and harvest *kumash-ekwa*, the wood of oyster mushroom. Another example is found in Kwilekwaheel, a name that refers to Freddie Earl, who once built a trapper's cabin south from the mouth of Earl Creek. In fact, it is believed that Kwilekwaheel is probably the Nlaka'pamux name for that person, Freddie Earl, who spent time there. The general region here is a favourite place for getting *kumash*, or pine mushroom, in late spring and early fall and is remembered by the man who lived at the place.

Tsatzook, in Nlaka'pamux, literally means "red writings or markings" and refers to the almost two hundred rock paintings on an overhang above the river. This site is said to have been used by past Indian doctors, and the paintings are said to be shaman paintings. The place is believed to have power; the significance of this place is borne in the word *tsatzook*, which represents in oral memory the sum of what has gone on there. Kakawzik, the mountain called Mt. Roach by non-natives, is described by elders as an Indian college, where the young people trained for their supernatural power. According to the elders of the area, the name is derived from the Nlaka'pamux word meaning "leap" or "jump" and speaks of an event in mythological time when a giant jumped from a nearby mountain and landed on top of Kakawzik.

It is a named place that exemplifies the *poiesis* of body, self and world. The jumping in this passage is defined in terms of "a jumping off" and can be seen as "activational" (in phenomenology's extended bodily terms). This action refers to the scale and precipitousness of the landscape as it is fashioned and depicted in the local creation stories. It also speaks to the scale of the mythological ancestors immortalized here. The area is an important ritual spot for the Nlaka'pamux people, the reality of which has been captured in the name Kakawsik as a sacred place: a sacred mountain of personal wisdom and of ownmost possibility, in Nlaka'pamux terms.

Again we see an example of the co-incidence of body and world, flowing together in place names, in the named place Inzikikin — which means to "fall a log across" — and also serves for the name of Stryen Creek (Last Chance Creek), which flows down the flanks of Kakawzik. The Nlaka'pamux name refers to the log bridge used to cross over this creek where it meets the Stein. Nearby this site is the rock painting known locally as the "asking rock," the special place where Nlaka'pamux stopped to pray and to ask permission before carrying on into the Stein Valley; it is here they asked for safety. The rock represents the threshold to the valley, all that represented and the possibilities to be attained there. Inzikikin is a good example of how the body can be a location, a flowing river and a threshold between two areas; it is the infinite extended surfaces of body and world that is provisioned within named places and in the land's speaking out to poetically fill the silence that is, now, sonic articulatory space.

A *Poiesis* of Enfoldment Written on Rock

Pictographs, literally picture writing, is the term archaeologists use to describe paintings on rock surfaces with red paint derived from iron oxides. In many cases, they serve to record and honour the relationship between an aspirant and his or her *sne7m* (or power). As the location of the pictographs are vision questing sites, they have spiritual significance to the Nlaka'pamux people, and thus exact locations are not provided in this book. Instead, I have developed descriptive headings, which are not intended to be formal or recognized place names, nor are they archaeological designations.[2] According to Teit, who garnered information from late-nineteenth-century informants, rock paintings often marked special places on the land where powerful forces of nature were believed to be particularly potent and mysterious. Up until the present, Native peoples have travelled to these places and held vigils, fasted and prayed or performed exercises to acquire supernatural power. Some pictographs depict battles, but the majority of paintings were done in the process of spiritual training exercises. The paintings are said to be so powerful that no Aboriginal person would choose to camp near them. There are large numbers of these pictograph panels along the trail that follows Stein Creek.

Each pictograph tells a story about the experience that unfolded there, at a particular sacred place. They attest to a period of months spent in isolation in the forest in search for a guardian spirit in the form of a non-human being, and thus the rock pictures are the outward expression of an enfoldment between the individual and surrounding non-human forces. They frequently depict animal people — human-like animals and animal-like humans — or anthropomorphic heavenly bodies. such as the sun man. In every case, they speak to the occurrence of a given activity within a place and give lasting meaning and significance to that place through the process of body-world poetics. Below are some examples of how rock art sites within the Stein serve as an example of body-world poetics.

Up on a High Face

This is considered to be a Stein rock site, even though it is not found along the Stein River or on the reserve land. Geometric figures and human animals represent the vortex of human and non-human engagement, thus characterizing an enfoldment of body and world. The painting depicts two grizzly bear tracks and a representation of a thunderbird; both animals represent guardian spirits of shamans and warriors (Teit 1900: 354). There may also be a Christian cross, a symbol found at several sites up the Stein. Chinese writing is also found on certain panels — the work of Chinese miners who lived in the area from 1860 to the 1930s. We see the Chinese inscription for "clear or clean water" (Lepofsky 1988, in Stein Valley Nlaka'pamux Heritage Park 1997).

Asking Rock

Locally known as "the asking rock," this is perhaps the best-known pictograph site in the Stein. It is located not far from the head of the Stein River Heritage Trail, just past the confluence of Styne (Last Chance) and Stein Creeks. The paintings here are located inside two water worn niches in a large granite outcrop. A traditional prayer, offering respect and asking for protection, is made at this site before entering the Stein. Thus, it is called "asking rock." If you stand on a low outcrop below the painting, there are distinctive echoes coming from the hollow, indicating a sound/meaning relationship. In this case, the site's auditory factors contribute to the symbolic meaning and provide an example of *poiesis* of place as a ratio of the senses. Charles Hill-Tout, as well as more recent Native narrators, tells us that certain hollowed places were made there by seekers of shamanic powers during their exercises, all down through the ages. Inside the largest painted hollow are two natural stone beds, which youths, during puberty rituals, used to lie upon. The place was also used by women while giving birth (Willy Dick in Lepofsky 1988, in Stein Valley Nlaka'pamux Heritage Park 1997).

Teit includes discussion with his Nlaka'pamux informants on the paintings at this site. He was told that the large bulbous figure with antlers or flowing hairs represents a vision, and the pair of wavy horizontal lines in the background was trails. The two circles connected by a single line are said to represent lakes connected by a river. This panel also depicts an entire enfoldment of human and non-human agents. There is an owl with outstretched wings sheltering a snake, animals, human figures, lightning, a mountain goat, the sun and a crescent moon. The painting also includes a boat-like structure and a Christian cross, plus a mountain goat beneath a painting of three lakes with creeks running out of them.

Prominent horizontal and vertical lines inside a hollow at Asking Rock could represent actual trails in the Stein, but they could also represent dream trails of hunters or shamans. Shamans could travel the trails to the land of the shades (or the dead) and using a shortcut, intercept a lost soul owned by a living person (Teit 1900: 342). Other less obvious paintings are also featured at this site (see York, Daly and Arnett 1993). Asking Rock is the most accessible rock painting in the Stein Valley and now, unfortunately, shows signs of vandalism.

Several Kilometres up the Stein Trail

There is a complex set of rock paintings starting about four kilometres up the Stein River Heritage Trail, in the place known as Devil's Staircase — for it resembles a staircase. The Nlaka'pamux name for this site is Ts'ets'ekw, meaning "markings," and it features the greatest concentration of pictographs in the Stein Valley. High above the two main pictograph sites is the waterfall of Christina Creek, which falls over a rock face above a deep overhang. According to Teit's early report (1990), waterfalls were the haunts of "mysteries." This site also may signify a sonic and acoustical *poiesis* as it incorporates the cascading waterfall into the poetic effect achieved through viewing, thus adding to its significance.

Group of Six Paintings

The paintings at this site are found in six groups. They are painted beneath overhangs with ledges and continue 85 metres upstream along the faces of tall cliffs. They are the furthest downstream set of rock writings at Ts'ets'ékw and are "separated from the roaring rapids by a stretch of boulders, pools and twisted piles of driftwood" (York, Daly and Arnett 1993: 94). One of the paintings is thought to represent a number of things: a woman, four grizzly bear tracks arranged around a mountain goat mountains and glaciers in valleys (a zig-zag design). Two of the paintings appear to refer to the nearby Christina Creek waterfall, which falls down high above this site, adding to its aesthetic significance. A strange figure created by two circles attached by a thick bar represented "lakes connected by a river," according to Teit. There is also a representation of a fish. "Single human figures, grizzly bear tracks, mountains and glaciers in valleys, mountain goats, cascades, lakes connected by rivers, and visions are the subject matter identified at this site by native informants over the last century" (Arnett in Lepofsky 1988: 48, in Stein Valley Nlaka'pamux Heritage Park 1997).

Above the Old Aboriginal Trail

A small grouping of pictographs is located above the old Aboriginal trail between two other pictograph sites and was found in July 1988 by archaeologist Chris Arnett. Just before the second site, there is a small, moss-covered, granite overhang several metres above the old trail near the river. Small cedar trees populate the area. On a smooth face underneath the overhang are tiny pictographs, "painted with very thin lines suggestive of tiny fingers on a brush" (York, Daly and Arnett 1993: 110), featuring bird-like figures and mountain goats. Mountain goats were a frequent guardian spirit of women. Arnett speculates that this is likely a women's spot, due to the subject matter and the fine lines that characterize the paintings. More inquiry may or may not indicate a positive relationship between female paintings and delicate rendering, which would designate the site as a female power site, possibly also because of earlier events there.

Very Large Painting Site

One of the largest painting sites in Canada, it is located upstream from the group of six paintings. It runs for a distance of 120 metres at the base of a towering cliff and contains over 160 individual pictographs. The rock paintings appear on fallen slabs, under overhangs, on boulders and on faces of vertical rock. The Nlaka'pamux name for this place is Ts'ets'ekw, and it is a location familiar to many of the people. The position of the cliff in relation to the rushing river causes the pleasant acoustic effect common to other Stein pictograph sites — namely, "a continuous wash of white noise" (Arnett in Lepofsky 1988: 51; Stein Valley Nlaka'pamux Heritage Park 1997). This acoustical dimension likely speaks to another site of sound/meaning relationships, as mentioned above. Shirley James, an Nlaka'pamux person from Lytton, was told by her grandmother that the site was used by Indian doctors and, therefore, has special significance because of their activities. Several rock-lined fireplaces are evident in the sandy cedar grove, strewn with boulders between the river and the cliff site, indicating human activity. The paintings include forty mountain goats, twelve two-headed snakes, eleven deer, six horned lizards, five owls and five grizzly bear tracks, as well as skeletons, grave poles, male and female humans, suns, crescent moons, rib-cages, trails and rivers with trees along them, generally depicting a swirl of nature and a vision site. One of the paintings at this site might represent a "battle pictograph," depicting a battle between the Lil'wat of Mt. Currie and the Nlaka'pamux. Two nail-headed warriors carrying bows and shields are depicted next to a painting of a river lined with trees. There is also a human male figure that appears to be firing a short-barrelled gun from the hip (Arnett in Lepofsky 1988; Stein Valley Nlaka'pamux Heritage Park 1997). At least one such battle was said to have taken place in the Stein at Scudmore Creek.

Weather-Worn Figure

This site consists of one pictograph, of a single weather-worn figure on the side of a large, three metre high granite boulder close to the trail, near the river. Much of the painting has been worn away. The large figure has spread wings on the side of a giant boulder and is six kilometres from the head of the Stein Heritage Trail. The painting, just a few metres from the trail, is highly visible to all who pass by. It was identified in July 1988 by Brian Molyneaux and Chris Arnett. According to Nlaka'pamux elder Annie York, the painting depicts the double-headed snake representing death, which is the hunter's power figure, with a headdress, bowl and cup (York Daly and Arnett 1993: 3).

Twenty Large Paintings

The paintings depict several long diagonal lines and two male figures with bows and nail-shaped heads — who seem to be hunting young deer or goats. Also depicted are other nail-headed humans, a small animal with a spear through its body, a thunderbird and a grizzly bear track (York, Daly and Arnett 1993: 167). These are associated with puberty rites and have special significance for the locals because they are iconic representations on the spiritual or religious events that took place here, as explained above in the passages on puberty ceremonies.

Large Boulder, Upstream from Weather-Worn Figure

Upstream from weather-worn figure is a large boulder with an interesting, womb-like shelter hollowed into it by the action of the water and rock. Inside this shelter, along the east wall, are paintings of bright red. They depict men with game animals, horizontal lines, large fish, a torso with arms and a rib cage. Also, a thunderbird and a human figure in a conical hat are found at the entrance. Above the entrance way is a potbellied thunderbird figure with an upside-down human underneath its beak. The paintings suggest this to be a vision cave used by shamans. The body-word poetics present in this site encompass the unique womb-like formation, the curious movement of the water, the bright paintings and their positioning and the abiding statement of what is done there.

Above the Rushing River

At least twenty-five pictographs appear on rock faces for a distance of 75 metres, above the rushing river where the Stein Heritage Trail dips close to the river's edge. The panel represents a maritime motif that obviously indicates familiarity with the coast. Corner speculates that the paintings might be a two-masted schooner, complete with figurehead, furled sails and crow's nest. It has also been interpreted as two men in a large Haida or Nootka dugout canoe (Corner 1968: 16). On further speculation, the painting likely depicts a Salish canoe with two paddlers and a carved animal bow figure. The site also includes two representations of what possibly are graves with Christian crosses, a series of dots which represent stars, a frontal figure with outstretched arms, a pot-belly and feathered headdress, a human figure and a lynx communicating (explaining the personhood of animals and the enfoldment of humans into the non-human world) and a depiction of what is likely a "dream trail," or an actual trail. Above these is an alcove overlooking the Stein, featuring a row of four deer, one mountain goat, three types of rib cages, groups of game animals along diagonal lines and an abstract cross.

Low Boulder

Faint, linear lines of paint appear on the side of an angular, low boulder close to the trail 12 kilometres from the head of the Stein River Heritage Trail, on the north side of the river. Lichen has obscured most of this panel (Arnett in Lepofsky 1988; Stein Valley Nlaka'pamux Heritage in Park 1997). The remains of a cabin are also visible across the river from this site. Ethnographically, this rock marks the start of a region well-known as a gathering site for cedar root for basket making, indicating what human activity has occurred there. According to elder Annie York, it's likely a woman's site: "These are women's things here. That's a digging stick on the left. That Sun Man told them that a woman's instrument is not going to be the bow and arrow. It's just a stick like a hoe. That was his design but it wasn't comfortable to dig with" (York, Daly and Arnett 1993: 194). The depictions indicate this is likely a site of women's puberty ceremonies: when women received digging sticks. It is thought that the site's symbolism likely represents female harvesting activity.

Vision Cave Shelter

The large protected shelter created by large boulders features a painting of two faces — each with connected eyebrows and nose, large eyes and open mouths, who gesture with single arms and have mask-like faces. On the ceiling in the centre is a large natural stain of iron oxide. A game-like animal with prominent genitals leaps to one side; two diagonal lines represent its rib cage. On the east face of the large boulder are eight human-like figures in two groups. Some of the figures have large stomachs, heads and/or cone-shaped heads. The cone-shaped headdresses may represent the regalia used by shamans to travel to the land of the dead and thus would indicate a shaman site.

Five Orange Paintings

Five orange paintings adorn the base of a large boulder at the furthest up-river site of the Stein Valley. It is approximately 20 kilometres west of the confluence of the Stein and Fraser Rivers, on the north side of the river, close to the trail. There are conflicting interpretations of these paintings. Rousseau and Howe identified the painting as a horse and rider in 1979, but Arnett and Molyneaux, on further investigation, clarify that it is not a horse and rider but rather a solitary rayed arc, which could represent unfinished basketry, a motif adopted by young women during their puberty training (Arnett in Lepofsky 1988; Stein Valley Nlaka'pamux Heritage Park 1997). This, therefore, is likely a women's puberty spot. According to elder Annie York, the pictograph shows the Sun Man, the sun with a dot in the middle: "This means an eclipse is coming" (York, Daly and Arnett 1993: 214). She further tells that the rayed triangle over the boy's head is what he must wear to talk to the sun and that the rayed arc over the man is a bridge the boy must build; it is rayed because everything the boy builds must resemble the sun. According to the early ethnographers, the sun was a common guardian spirit for those wishing to be shamans or warriors. The relationship the boy has with the sun — as his extended bodily self — seems poetically expressive from the perspective of body-world representations.

Site Nine Hundred Metres above the Stein

Situated over 900 metres above the Stein River Heritage Trail, on the south side of the valley four kilometres above the cable crossing, is the most spectacular and inaccessible rock painting site in the Stein Valley. It is a painted cave located in 1986 by Wickwire, Lay and Nlaka'pamux elder Willie Justice. The pictographs occur on a south-facing rock face, west of the entrance, directly over the entrance and on its walls and ceilings. It also has a well-worn natural stone seat inside the entrance, which provides exquisite views of the valley, suggesting that it has been a viewpoint. Eleven depictions of mountain goats decorate the walls, while mountain goat dung covers the floor. The outside paintings depict thunderbird connected by a line to an animal with a spear shot through its back. Another animal is above it amid six large paint smears. Paintings over the entrance include a sunburst, a naked man and another animal with a spear in its back. Isolated geometric figures appear around the entrance and inside on the walls and on the ceiling. Figures of men, mountain goats, geometric figures and lines flow from walls to ceiling inside the cave, seeming to depict the flowing together of human and non-human elements (Wickwire in Elsey 1997: 17).

Unique Charcoal Pictograph

At this site, a unique charcoal pictograph is drawn upon the scar of a culturally modified cedar tree. According to I.R. Wilson, who officially recorded it, this is the only site of its kind in British Columbia, though paintings on trees are well documented in the ethnographic literature. Two scars made by native people are visible on the tree. The scar on the east side has an unidentified design made of small, shallow marks created by a small knife. Charcoal drawings occur on the west side of the tree. The drawings are a two-headed creature with deer antlers, a male human figure with large ears and horns, and a large single human form. Tree-ring data indicate that the bare scars on which the paintings are placed were caused by bark stripping done after 1875 and before 1907 (Parker, in M'Gonigle and Wickwire 1988: 9).

Rock Carving

The only known petroglyph, or rock carving, in the Stein watershed is on a large boulder, a metre high by a metre in diameter, located 200 metres south of the Stein and Fraser confluence, on Stryen Reserve No. 9. It was identified by David Sanger in September 1961, with information provided by Andrew Johnny Jr. of Stein. The boulder's west face portrays three human female figures. The left one has a prominent rib cage. Bird-like figures and the sun are also featured. The south face of the boulder depicts other abstract figures and a series of arches. Around the top of the rock are simple, pecked holes 4 centimetres in diameter and 2 centimetres deep (Bouchard and Kennedy, in Wilson 1988: 116). According to elder Annie York, the site depicts beetles and birds, but represents one story, about a boy's grandmother who said, "My eyes will be far out to watch over you. She was blind, that old lady. She had power and when you have it you can see things other people can't" (York, Daly, and Arnett 1993: 218).

Notes

1. The Stein Valley is known as a very important archaeological site mainly due to the great number of red ochre pictographs on the rock faces along the Stein River. Many of the panels are large and complex. Most of them were made by youths during their puberty rites as a method of honouring their guardian spirit or *sne7m*. Illustrations of these panels (an interpretation) can be found in *They Write Their Dreams on the Rock Forever* (York, Daly and Arnet 1993).
2. The exact location of these sites is the property of the Nlaka'pamux people, thus such information must be distributed by the Nlaka'pamux (Lytton) First Nation only and cannot be revealed within this text. The Stein pictographs are recorded archaeological sites with the standard Borden site designation.

Chapter 7

Being-on-the-Land and the Indigenous Experience

During the course of this study, I analyzed the issue of being-in-the-world within the ethnographic context among certain First Nations in British Columbia. I stretched this concept to encompass a variety of geographically situated meaningful goings on within what has been referred to as a traditional tribal territory. I demonstrated, through a review of the ethnographic folkloric accounts in British Columbia, that spaces inevitably result from areas of meaningful activity, or as places of dwelling, building and human creativity (Heidegger 1971: 154), as is seen, for example, in tales of the Yanyedi people on the Taku, or in the case of Mount Cheam for the Stó:lō people, or for the Statliumx and Nlaka'pamux on the southwestern plateau. I argue that the *poiesis* uncovered throughout the ethnographic literature results from the expressiveness which inheres within the activational relationship between "body and world" as a behavioural location. It is expressiveness, or speaking out, that is improvised and, therefore, continually adjusted anew in the dynamic and ongoing relationship between a people and their environment.

Throughout this book, the meaning of land is tied to the notion of Indigenous use but also to the presence of an Aboriginal poetics that anchors people to the land at the deepest level of human meaning, identity and culture. The folkloric interpretation of land as an expression of selfhood among the First Nations of British Columbia is important because the majority of First Nations existing within the province originally were not part of the federal/provincial treaty process at the time of Confederation and, thus, do not possess treaties. First Nations' claims throughout British Columbia are under legal scrutiny, which adds urgency to the argument that the meaning of tribal territory is integrally tied to Native selfhood and to an entire way of life, and thus cannot and should not be commodified. First Nations' identity across Canada has, for the last century, existed between two levels of experience: that of the colonized Native (living under the *Indian Act*) versus a life guided by the territorial customs and sensibilities typical of the traditional, Aboriginal hunter and fisher. The reality of First Nations life has, to a great extent, been placed out of view and become invisible to outsiders, a reality that is metaphorically suggested through the power and presence of the "white man's maps" (Brody 1981).

In spite of the initiatives of the *Indian Act* to silence and homogenize the diverse First Nations voices and to dissolve the existing boundaries between the unique First Nations and the "whitestream," the Native maps and land use practices remain alive as testimony to a surviving Aboriginal way of life (Brody 1981; Denis 1997). Just as the authenticity of the First Nations' identity and existence in British Columbia has been obfuscated and obscured by the presence of white man's maps and utilitarian principles, so has the daily life, the identity and the true meaning of land been obfuscated by the *Indian Act*. Across the nation, the *Indian Act* unilaterally imposed a political, education and economic system upon the diverse First Nations people and cultures. The *Indian Act*, originally devised as a vehicle of control, education and assimilation of the diverse First Nations, served to homogenize First Nations people across Canada and to narrow First Nations' identity to fit the one inauthentic category of colonized "Indian." Thus, for more than a century, the diverse and culturally rich and distinct First Nations of Canada and of British Columbia existed largely unnoticed under a Euro-colonial grid of meaning and identity created and imposed by the government of Canada and the *Indian Act*.

Consequently, the process of Confederation truncated the Native experience into two distinct levels: that of the colonized person living under the *Indian Act* and that of the Native insider who still maintained a vibrant and authentic Aboriginal lifestyle within a culturally and spiritually rich tribal territory. Life and identity within First Nations territories, since the time of *Indian Act*, has largely been hidden by the two contrasting levels of existence that the Act created, which can be expressed as that of the public versus the private experience. One dimension of life can be summed up by the word "colonial," created by the political objectives of the federal government, the society at large, the *Indian Act* and the residential school system. The other dimension, the traditional life on the land, has been hidden from view but unequivocally still exists. Thus, at a time when treaties are in the making within British Columbia, it is important to emphasize the contrast between a shared life on the territory and the utilitarian, Eurocentric objectives that frequently infiltrate the discourses surrounding the clarification of section 35 of the Canadian Constitution, on Aboriginal rights.

If left uninformed, the dualistic and individualistic values inherent in neo-liberal (rationalist) discourses can perpetuate ethnocentric outcomes within Aboriginal title and rights forums, thus, re-focusing discussions on Aboriginal rights and justice back along colonial lines. In the early 1990s, a provincial court decision had already been appealed to the Supreme Court of Canada due to a colonial and ethnocentric error of judgment that occurred during an original decision in the resolution of the Gitxan and Wet'suwet'en land claims case, known as *Delgamuukw* (Culhane 1998). However, the true interpretation of section 35 can best occur within a non-dualistic, non-Western approach that valorizes oral traditions and the centrality of First Nations' stories, oral testimonies, dances and songs and artworks. Historically and to the present, the Aboriginal meaning of land, as signified by the term poetics, emerges directly from the territory, from traditional activities and use patterns, from the teaching of elders, from the oral traditions and from the age-old stories which are passed on from generation to generation and depict an authentic Fist Nations way of life. It is this *poiesis* that speaks to the life on the land, to the true meaning of the territory and to the self-identification between the people and their own environment, which can offer an authentic site of resistance against re-colonization from more insidious forms of colonialism, world order and globalization. It is through looking at the land in a non-dualistic and more embodied way that the true meaning of land for the diverse First Nations can start to be revealed.

The *poiesis*, or the body's own expressiveness (as has been shown throughout the analysis of diverse ethnographic regions within British Columbia), can be found in the many symbols and representations of the First Nations within their territories. *Poiesis* gives testimony to a story that has been mapped onto a territorial background on the basis of human doing and, therefore, is indicative of human possibility and productivity — as being-in-the-world.

The Aboriginal place names, landmarks, ancestral locations, narratives, vision sites, power spots and so on are themes for bodily activity and meaning, and constitute a storyscape that demonstrates authentic territorial activity and meaning. Meaningful places on the land, as narratively encoded, are the recognizable poles of action, as was seen in the transformer rock Xeyxelemos at Sweetie's camp on the Fraser River in Stó:lō territory. The poetics of dwelling, seen in the landmarks and their stories presented throughout this book, were also found in many diverse aesthetic forms of territorial representation and expression (such as crests and songs, dances, etc.) that express special or sacred territorial sites or are the places of origin for a given people. The chapters in this book present ethnographic examples from five different Indigenous settings to demonstrate how a formulation of body-world *poiesis* is conceptually useful in analyzing Aboriginal representations and narrative forms towards an understanding of Aboriginal, territorial dwelling. I looked at five examples: 1. the coastal culture area; 2. the Lower Stl'atl'imx' territory (the Lillooet River); 3. the Upper Stl'atl'imx' territory; 4. the Nlaka'pamux tribal territory; and 5. the Stein Valley Nlaka'pamux Tribal Heritage Park. All provide examples of the *poiesis* of body and world and serve as storyscapes that present representations of Aboriginal real dwelling as embedded in *poiesis*. The ethnographic examples of the Lower

Stl'atl'imx', the Upper Stl'atl'imx', the Nlaka'pamux and the Nlaka'pamux Stein provide a wide range of examples of body-world *poiesis* in the form of mythological landmarks, which speak to human presencing as an extended self. The territorial stories, songs and dances based on the many territorial traditions (such as the songs, family crests and regalia discovered in the cases of the Gitxan, the Kwageulth and the Nuu-chah-nulth coastal tribes) illustrate the notion of the extended body as poetic and aesthetic expression. The book also illustrates the relationship between the folklore scholarly theories of being-in-the-world, by drawing attention to the connection between the aesthetic representations (landmarks, rocks art, crests, stories, etc.) and various territorial meanings and activities that give rise to them. Many such aesthetic representations of dwelling were found, for example, in the Stein Valley, where rock art sites, landmarks and named places show the activational relationship between people and place (land), which has been symbolically represented through a narrative or symbolic (repetitive) means.

The examples throughout this book clearly demonstrate that the network of meaningful places that constitute a territorial dwelling have an ancestral foundation that was established by the travel patterns of the early ancestors and thus represent the oral maps of the former ancestral territorial practices. In other words, the early tribal networks between people (such as family-owned harvesting sites, fishing spots and territorial borders) have been inscribed in the folklore and, co-incidentally thereby, on the land. In the case of both coastal and interior peoples' traditions, the folkloric defining of landscape as the poetics of their activity and self-identification was a leading feature in the oral traditions. Therefore, for the legendary traditions of these regions (Kwageulth, Gitxan, Tsimshian, Tlingit, Nuu-chah-nulth, Stó:lō, Nlaka'pamux, Statliumx, Secwepemc, Lil'wat and Lower Lillooet), the narratives are contextualized geographically on the basis of well-known use sites within the territory that are marked-out physically on the basis of the oral narratives. The oral traditions, customs and narratives thematize the territory in such a way that allows for the self's possibility as meaningfully anchored as being-in-the-world at important and well-known places on the land. The poetic and symbolic gestures given in the narratives, such as place names, landmarks and rock paintings are what might be described as the containers of human activity, as it has unfolded and as it enfolds the land in the age-old sense — thus, they can be seen as the indicators of Aboriginal dwelling.

Throughout the ethnographic accounts, we constantly find self-identifying elements such as songs, narratives and other aesthetic traditions that originate from certain places on the land, which seem to speak out on life and define ancestral occurrences and which are constitutive of what is considered one's own. Thus, the territorial spatiality and the worldly presence of humans (as is formative of selfhood in phenomenological terms) emerges within the Aboriginal cultures of British Columbia as a compendium of aesthetic representations and communicative forms. Expressive of the territory, these poetic representational forms emerge from the human habitat within a specific territorial, geographical location, or what might be called a human "contexture," or background. As such, they speak to the issues of meaningful dwelling, or the territorial ethos of living and working together within a territorial home.

The stories looked at in this book clearly demonstrate (in the wider ethnographic context) the respect and self-identification that Aboriginals feet toward their land. It can be summed up as an undying attachment to their land, an abiding wish and heart-felt concern not to be alienated from it, as it is their own embodiment. Furthermore, the exploration of the above ethnographic accounts uncovers an expressed folkloric presence of the imbrication of humans and territories that speaks to an enfoldment of all human and non-human elements on the land, as an unbroken aroundness of being. As the discussions on the various First Nations of British Columbia show, the integration of all human and non-human elements in a shared life process has led to a generally ascribed personhood that is narratively depicted on the landscape. Similar poetic representations often take the form of geological formations and prominent mountains, as seen for the Stó:lō and others, and of animal beings in the case of the Gitxan. Such poetic renderings are demonstrated for all non-human agents — as found in the stories of Charlie Mack — who generally are seen to share a place within the same habitat and ethos of survival and communicative world as humans (Mack in Kennedy and Bouchard 2010; Cove 1987a, Scott 1989: 130).

Through the renderings of the many diverse ethnographic accounts, this discussion demonstrates the presence of a non-dualistic Aboriginal perspective to land and delineates the self-identification of Aboriginal people of British Columbia with their territories as their own "field of self." The Aboriginal poetics of land, as demonstrated throughout the collective folklore of British Columbia First Nations, is shown to be both spatially and spiritually indispensable for the First Nations people, who are anchored meaningfully as selves through the tribal territories' many narratives. The narratives and poetic/symbolic gestures are indispensable in the maintenance and continuation of an Aboriginal moral world, and in the continuation of a First Nations' selfhood.

The creation stories and associated songs serve to define a given group's or individual's specific territorial and land use rights as inscribed ancestrally. Song, dances and stories, thus meaningfully position the person on the land in intergenerational and poetic terms. They are the vehicles in the double-edged purpose of enabling the self's presencing and, also, in anchoring what could be looked upon as the moral or human world.

The various ethnographic accounts in this book show the Aboriginal hunter-gatherer folkloric and poetic depictions of the world to be representational of a complete or non-dualistic world, as opposed to one that is disembodied or dismembered. The latter describes the dualistic world norms typical for western rationalist (Cartesian-based) societies, which tend to oppose self and world, nature and culture, human and non-human, and self and other as their dominant ontological foundation. This study uncovers the Aboriginal perspective of self as one flowing together with the non-human world, in which hunter-gatherers interact with the non-human beings and processes of their environment in an intimately connected and non-dualistic sense. Phenomenology's discourse is usefully employed in discussions on the Aboriginal perspective. The complementary between the Aboriginal perspective and the phenomenological perspective is found in the related categories of body, self and world, which is fundamentally in counterpoint to the mainstream, socially scientific discussions within the fields of anthropology, sociology, environmental studies, political economy and Aboriginal studies. Such dualistic, scientistic approaches embrace viewpoints that oppose the categories of nature and culture and body-world, thus debarring the domain of personhood from all non-human agents and animals and violating Aboriginality as a perspective wherever they are applied to the topic of Native rights, culture or Aboriginal land and territories.

The Aboriginal aesthetic and symbolic illustrations drawn upon for the purposes of this book discredit the scientistic dichotomies of nature and culture, as they demonstrate that it is the body's sensuous interactions and incorporation with a non-human world in the Aboriginal context that leads to the emergence of a meaningful and narratively articulated world. It is rather the human figure's capacity and necessity to be meaningfully situated or anchored bodily (and spatially) in its purposes and movements which sustains and gives rise to the many symbolic or narrative forms traditionally known as culture (Zaner 1981: 171). First Nations' folkloric representations, drawn from the various groups under study, relate to the ability to meaningfully address the world and to be locationally situated in terms of productivity, possibility, activity and belonging within a territorial world context. To be anchored spatially is necessary to function meaningfully and to operate in a productive way within a meaningfully appointed behavioural setting. The many representations that flow from life's journey speak to the self's capability to do just that and to the multi-faceted enterprise of being-in-the-world as an environmentally and culturally placed human.

The Aboriginal folkloric perspective under discussion shows the self to be the product of an enfoldment of body and world, as well as the accompanying imbrication of both human and non-human agents as its own experiential unfolding (Evernden 1985; Ingold 1996; Merleau-Ponty 1968). The immersed viewpoint of phenomenology and the notion of the extended body as self have been useful in locating the Aboriginal folklore within a well-known scholarly discourse of non-dualism. The interconnected categories of body, self and world, which legitimate and valorize the Aboriginal perspective for its inherent philosophical, environmental, aesthetic and humanistic value, assist in moving the Aboriginal peoples' worldview on self and land into the arena of scholarly discussion.

This book demonstrates how the phenomenological view on the imbrication between self and world — as an interconnected process — is useful in illuminating the non-dualistic approach in the worldview represented in B.C. First Nations' oral traditions, symbolism and folklore. The non-dualist tradition of European phenomenology, through the works of Maurice Merleau-Ponty, Martin Heidegger, Richard Zaner and others as well as Neil Evernden and other environmental phenomenologists, complements and serves as the academic ally to a growing body of Indigenous scholarship and to the regional and ancestral stories of the Native people of British Columbia.

A further objective of this book is to valorize, legitimate and emphasize the environmental awareness and respect of the Aboriginal traditional approach by showing how Aboriginal territorial affiliations have manifested in a system of authentic dwelling and environmental care of both human and non-human components inhering within the tribal territory. The respectfulness for place and for the territorial lands associated with care, belonging and possibility of a given people are, thus, galvanized and observable in the Aboriginal folklore in British Columbia and in the many aesthetic forms, such as stories, sonic articulatory forms, local landmarks, symbolism (masks and crests) and rituals such as dances and songs.

Implicit in Maurice Merleau-Ponty's argument that "the body has its world" is the realization that the non-human world actually becomes formulated as our own embodiment — that is, the world as the ratio of the senses. Through the analysis of the folkloric ethnographic accounts, the Aboriginal folkloric worldview is shown to correspond to territorial movement and activities. Thus, a complementarity is demonstrated between phenomenology and the Aboriginal viewpoint. The three-fold structure of enfoldment, storyscape and *poiesis* shows the relationship between the non-dualistic imbrication of Aboriginal peoples and their territory and explains the resonance of such an imbrication at the level of folkloric representation and selfhood. Through this structure, it is possible to demonstrate how representations and expressions — as found within the Aboriginal worldview — are manifestations of the extended non-dualistic self and, thus, on an iconic level, speak to the issue of human dwelling; they speak to the ethos of what happens in the territory.

The three-fold structure of enfoldment, storyscape and *poiesis* thus presents a three-fold analysis of the extended self in the Aboriginal context.

The conceptual level of enfoldment speaks to body-world imbrication as an experience of the territory. The conceptual level of storyscape speaks to the territorial experiences and activities of the lived body as manifested in narrative terms, as world emergence and as the moral and meaningful positioning of people on the land. The conceptual level of *poiesis* captures the relationship between humans and their world as made manifest through the many aesthetic representations that frame those experiences within a narrative context and give them meaning. *Poiesis* is the world as a ratio of the senses as it emerges in poetic form and is narratively framed, as it is communicable cultural expression. *Poiesis* is the iconic reflexivity of the extended self within the world context. It is at the level of *poiesis* that the lessons of culture and of real dwelling are lived and communicated, through the poetic representations of body and world, as have received narrative significance and moral gravity within a specific territorial dwelling. The three-fold structure, thus, emphasizes the complementarity between the folkloric Aboriginal worldview and phenomenology through finding like themes between the two traditions on the relationship of body and world and on the ethos of human dwelling.

The illustration of the many Aboriginal storyscapes offer a meaningful point of access for outsiders to First Nations' communities for grasping and appreciating the Aboriginal perspective on the world as one which is lived and manifested within a territorial surrounding. The recognition of storyscapes relating to regional landscapes as poetic/aesthetic representations with a corresponding matrix of ecoscapes and use-sites, special and charged places, etc., provides a meaningful tool in the joint project of both Aboriginal and territorial preservation as a humanitarian priority. The regional storyscape represents nothing less than an environing *poiesis* of body and world. As such, the poetic and symbolic forms looked at provide the opportunity to uncover a meaningful approach to life for a people whose connection to the land is self-defining in the deepest sense and whose honouring and respect for the land represents a worldview that is not cut off from the non-human processes that sustain them to the extent that — at some level — the human and the non-human worlds are eminently relatable as being one.

Glossary

anti-Cartesian: schools of thought that oppose Enlightenment thinking, or rationalist, scientific reasoning, such as emerged with the writing of Descartes during the "age of reason." Such critiques deconstruct epistemological paradigms incumbent on the opposition of subject and object.

assimilation: similar to homogenization, assimilation is the process of erasing the specific identity and autonomy of a unique, minority peoples, thus bringing about their absorption into wider mainstream culture.

being-on-the-land: conceptualizes identity as primarily a situational or positional phenomenon such that being and significance largely reflects one's social and geographical surroundings.

Cartesian: refers to a turn of mind, or set of epistemological principles, that stem from the writing of Rene Descartes, an Enlightenment scholar believed to be the originator of scientific rationalism.

colonialism: an economic and political process which brings about the domination of a pre-existing and resident group of people by either an external nation or power, or by a population of newcomers or settlers.

cultural genocide: speaks to the destruction of an Indigenous culture through a process of colonial rule.

decolonization: a process undertaken by governments to root-out internal, colonial process in order to honour the United Nations Declaration on the Rights of Indigenous Peoples and to accomplish reconciliation with colonized peoples within the borders of the nation state.

enfoldment: addresses the issue of the spatiality of the lived body as a ratio of the senses. It is the relationship between body and world, through which the body is experienced as an extended body encompassing all that it touches, moves through and experiences.

ethnocentric: within social science this term including value judgments of a cultural or ethnic other by an outside observer. For the purposes of this text, the concept is used to describe Western or hegemonic methods of interpreting the world and thus is critical of European/Western viewpoints on nature, law, government, ethics, institutions and morality which are imposed on Indigenous peoples.

existential: drawn from the philosophy of existentialism and addresses that which pertains to personal existence and experience. It generally refers to the phenomenon of personhood, as that which relates to the experience of being a person.

extended body: relates to the self as a field of environmental awareness, experience and expression.

field of self: a phenomenological term that addresses the matter of holism and the notion that bodies cannot be viewed as separate, atomistic entities, but rather are an experiential centre for the expression of the surrounding world. Thus, the physical self and its surrounding world are seen as an unbroken continuum or field.

homogenization: the process of erasing the cultural specificity of a regional population, thus causing the subsumption of the unique or ethnically separate group into a wider cultural category or mainstream population.

iconical/iconic: refer to poetic expressions of the lived body which speak to historical experiences of a culture as a whole.

non-Cartesian: refers to modes of thought or experience that either pre-date the onset of Western rationalism, or represent experiential modes of thought which do not embrace rationalist, scientific paradigms and mathematical ways of knowing.

non-dualistically: refers to a worldview that subscribes neither to the dualities of Cartesian thought nor to the epistemological propositions of Western rationalism.

Occidental self: encapsulates the traits of personal identity of the European Enlightenment Period, which is generally characterized by individualism, rationalism and Western academic or economic consciousness.

ontological: the study of being. For the purposes of this book, ontology contrasts and opposes epistemology, that is, the study of knowledge and the theoretical foundations of science.

personhood: the experience and state of being a person.

phenomenology: a branch of European philosophy on the study of meaning and being as it relates to the spatiality of the lived body and how it creates its world as a shared, symbolic world of human and social significance.

poiesis: originally drawn from the philosophers Aristotle and Heidegger, it means poetry or poetics. It is used throughout this book to refer to the symbolic expressions of the lived body as they emerge directly from experience.

selfhood: represents the domain of the self as an existentially, meaningful idea or phenomenon.

storyscape: addresses a geographical region that represents a cultural world by virtue of its meaningful, poetic and storied significance based on the historical tellings of regional events.

utilitarian: refers to a point of view associated with liberalism, which establishes the ultimate value and importance of all worldly things in terms of their mathematical economic value.

Select Bibliography

Abram, D. 1996. *The Spell of the Sensuous*. New York, NY: Pantheon Books.

Absolon, K. (Minogiizhigokwe). 2011. *Kaandossiwin: How We Come to Know*. Halifax, NS: Fernwood Press.

Adams, J.W. 1973. *The Gitxan Potlatch*. Toronto, ON: Holt, Rinehart and Winston of Canada Ltd.

Alfred, T. 2009a. *Peace, Power, Righteousness: An Indigenous Manifesto*. Toronto, ON: Oxford University Press.

____. 2009b. "Sovereignty: An Inappropriate Concept." In R. Maaka and C. Andersen (eds.), *The Indigenous Experience*. Toronto, ON: Canadian Scholar Press.

Amoss, P.T. 1978. *Coast* Salish *Spirit Dancing*. Seattle, WA: University of Washington Press.

____. 1977. "Strategies of Reorientation: The Contribution of Contemporary Winter Dancing to Coast Salish Identity and Solidarity." *Arctic Anthropology* 14, 1.

Anderson, A.C. 1846. "Journal For An Expedition--Hudson's Bay Company Archives." Manitoba, B.97/A/3.

Aristotle. 1961. *Aristotle's Poetics*. Translated by S.H. Butcher, introduction by Francis Fergussen. New York, NY: Hill and Wang.

Armstrong, J. 2007. *Slash*. Penticton, BC: Theytus Press.

____. 2006. "Sharing One Skin." *Cultural Survival Quarterly* 30, 4 (Land and Resources in the Americas). Posted June 9, 2010 at <www.culturalsurvival.org/publications/cultural-survival-quarterly/canada/sharing-one-skin>.

____. 2005a. *A Radically Different World View Is Possible: The Gift Economy Inside and Out of Patriarchal Capitalism*. Las Vegas, NV: International Conference on the Gift Economy.

____. 2005b. I Stand With You Against Disorder. *Ues! Online, Winter*. <http://www.gifteconomyconference.com/pages/Armstrong.html>.

____. 2000. *Whispering in Shadow*. Penticton, BC: Theytus Press.

____. 1999. "Let Us Begin With Courage: Blowing Drifts Moon." In Armstrong et al. *Ecoliteracy: Mapping the Terrain*. Centre for Eco-Literacy.

Armstrong, J., and D. Cardinal. 1992. *The Native Creative Process*. Penticton, BC: Theytus Books.

Atleo, R. 2004. *Tsawalk: A Nuu-chah-nulth Worldview*. Vancouver, BC: UBC Press.

Asch, M. 1993. *Home and Native Land: Aboriginal Rights and the Canadian Constitution*. Vancouver, BC: UBC Press.

____. 1990. *Aboriginal Self Government and Canadian Constitutional Identity: Building Reconciliation in Ethnicity and Aboriginality*. Toronto, ON: University of Toronto Press.

B.C. Parks (Ministry of Environment, Lands, and Parks, Parks Division). 1997. "Stein Valley Nlaka'pamux Heritage Park, A Provincial Park." In *Management Planning Background Document*. Victoria, BC.

Bakhtin, M. 1993. *Toward a Philosophy of Act*. Translated by Vadim Liapunov, edited by Michael Holquist. Austin, TX: University of Texas Press.

Baskin, Cindy. 2006. "Aboriginal World Views as Challenges and Possibilities in Social Work Education." *Critical Social Work* 7.

Basso, K. 1996. *Wisdom Sits in Places: Landscape and Language among the Western Apache*. Albuquerque, NM: University of New Mexico Press.

____. 1984. *Stalking the Stories: Names, Places, and Moral Narratives among the Western Apache, in Text, Play and Story: The Construction and Reconstruction of Self and Society*. Proceedings of the Anthropological Ethnological Society, edited by Edward Bruner. Seattle, WA: Washington Anthropological Association.

____. 1992. *Speaking with Names: Language and Landscape among the Western Apache, in Rereading Cultural Anthropology.* Edited by George E. Marcus. Durham and London: Duke University Press.

Behr, T. 2009. "Indigenous Voice and a Colony Re-Imagined." A paper presented at the Annual General Meeting of the Canadian Anthropological Society. University of British Columbia, May.

Belanger, Y. 2010. *Ways of Knowing: An Introduction to Native Studies in Canada.* Toronto, ON: Nelson Education.

Bentley, M., and T. Bentley. 1981. *Gabriola: Petroglyph Island.* Victoria, BC: Sono Nis Press.

Bierwert, C. 1999. *Brushed by Cedar, Living by the River: Coast Salish Figures of Power.* Tucson, AZ: University of Arizona Press.

Boas, F. 1969a. *The Religion of the Kwakiutl Indians, Volumes (1) and (2).* New York, NY: AMS Press.

____. 1969b. *Geographical Names of the Kwakiutl Indians.* New York, NY: AMS Press.

____ (ed.). 1969 [1917]. *Folk-Tales of Salishan and Sahaptin Tribes.* Volume 11. Lancaster, PA and New York, NY: American Folk-Lore Society.

____. 1966a. *The Winter Ceremonial in Indians of the North Pacific Coast.* Edited by Tom McFeat. Toronto, ON: McClelland and Stewart.

____. 1966b. *Kwakiutl Ethnography.* Chicago, IL: University of Chicago Press.

____. 1916. *The Social Organization and the Secret Societies of the Kwakiutl Indians.* New York, NY: Johnson Reprint Corp.

____. 1897. "The Decorative Art of the Indians of the North Pacific Coast of America." *Bulletin of the American Museum of Natural History* 9.

____. 1895. "Fifth Report on the Indians of British Columbia." 65th Report of the British Association for the Advancement of Science, p. 522–92.

____. 1894. "The Indian Tribes of the Lower Fraser River." 64th Report of the British Association for the Advancement of Science for 1890, p. 454–63.

Bouchard, R., and D. Kennedy. 1998. "Lillooet." In *Handbook of North American Indians, Vol. 12: Plateau.* Washington, DC: Smithsonian Institution.

____. 1988 [1985]. "Indian Land Use and Indian History of the Stein River Valley, British Columbia." Report prepared for I.R. Wilson Consultants Ltd. and B.C. Forest Products Ltd. Victoria, BC: Heritage Conservation Branch.

____ (eds.). 1979. *Shuswap Stories.* Vancouver, BC: CommCept Publishing.

____ (eds.). 1977. "Lillooet Stories." *British Columbia Sound History (Aural History Series)* 6, 1. Victoria, BC: British Columbia Archives.

____. 1971. "Lillooet Stories." *Manuscript, British Columbia Indian Language Project.* Victoria, BC.

Brealey, K.G. 1995. "Mapping Them 'Out': Euro-Canadian Cartography and the Appropriation of the Nuxalk and Tsi'ilqot'in First Nations' Territories, 1793–1916." *Canadian Geographer* 39, 2: 140–56.

Brody, Hugh. 1981. *Maps and Dreams.* Vancouver, BC: Douglas and McIntyre.

Brown, L., and S. Strega. 2005. *Research as Resistance: Critical, Indigenous, and Anti-Oppressive Approaches.* Toronto, ON: Canadian Scholar Press.

Carlson, K. 2010. *The Power of Place, the Problem of Time: Aboriginal Identity and Historical Consciousness in the Cauldron of Colonialism.* Toronto, ON: University of Toronto Press.

____. 1997. *You Are Asked to Witness.* Chilliwack, BC: Stó:lō Heritage Trust.

Carlson, K.T., S. McHalsie and D. Shaepe. 2001. *A Stó:lō Coast Salish Historical Atlas.* Vancouver, BC: Douglas and McIntyre.

Chamberlain, J. 2003. *If This Is Your Land, Where Are Your Stories? Finding Common Ground.* Toronto, ON: A.A. Knopt Canada.

Chatwin, B. 1987. *The Songlines.* New York, NY: Penguin Books.

Clifford, J. 1988. *The Predicament of Culture: Twentieth-Century Ethnography, Literature, and Art.* Cambridge, MA: Harvard University Press.

Clifford, J., and G. Marcus (eds.). 1986. *Writing Culture: The Poetics and Politics of Ethnography.*

Berkeley, CA: University of California Press.

Comaroff, John, and Jean Comaroff. 2009. *Ethnicity Inc*. University of Chicago Press.

Corner, J. 1968. *Pictographs (Indian Rock Paintings) in the Interior of British Columbia*. Vernon, BC: Wayside Press.

Couture, J. 1991. "Explorations in Native Knowing." In J. Friesen (ed.), *The Cultural Maze: Complex Question on Native Destiny in Western Canada*. Calgary, AB: Detselig Enterprises.

Cove, J. 1987a. *Tsimshian Narratives*. Collected by Marius Barbeau and William Beynon, edited by John Cove and George F. McDonald. Ottawa, ON: Canadian Museum of Civilization.

___. 1987b. *Shattered Images, Dialogues and Meditations on Tsimshian Narratives*. Ottawa, ON: Carleton University Press.

___. 1985. *A Detailed Inventory of the Barbeau Northwest Coast Files*. Ottawa, ON: National Museum of Man.

___. 1982. "The Gitxan Traditional Concept of Land Ownership." *Anthropologica* XXIV.

Cruikshank, J. 2005. *Do Glaciers Listen? Local Knowledge, Colonial Encounters and Social Imagination*. Vancouver, BC: UBC Press.

___. 1998. *The Social Life of Stories: Narrative and Knowledge in the Yukon Territory*. Vancouver, BC: UBC Press.

___. 1994. "Oral Tradition and Oral History: Reviewing Some Issues." *Canadian Historical Review* 75,3: 403–18.

___. 1992. "Invention of Anthropology in British Columbia's Supreme Court: Oral Tradition as Evidence in Delgamuukw v. B.C." *BC Studies* Autumn: 25–42.

___. 1990. "Getting the Words Right: Perspectives on Naming and Places in Athapaskan Oral History." *Arctic Anthropology* 27, 1.

Culhane, D. 1998. *The Pleasure of the Crown: Anthropology, Law and First Nations*. Vancouver, BC: Talonbooks.

Dawson, G. 1891. "Notes on the Shuswap People of British Columbia." In *Proceedings and Transactions of the Royal Society of Canada for the Year 1891: Sec. 1, Vol. 9*. Montreal.

De Laguna, F. 1972. *Under Mount St. Elias: The History and Culture of the Yakutat Tlingit*. Washington, DC: Smithsonian Contributions to Anthropology 7.

Denis, C. 1997. *We Are Not You, First Nations and Canadian Modernity*. Broadview, ON: Broadview Press.

DGNP (Dalgamuukw/Gisday'wa National Process). 1997. "An Initiative of the Assembly of First Nation's Office of the British Columbia Regional Vice Chief." <http://www.Delgamuukw.org/news/news.htm>.

Dickason, O. 2006. *A Concise History of Canada's First Nations*. New York, NY: Oxford University Press.

Dirlik, Arif. 1999. "Is There History After Eurocentrism: Globalism, Post-Colonialism and the Disavowal of History." *Cultural Critique* 42 (Spring).

___. 1996. "The Global in the Local." In R. Wilson and W. Dissanayake (eds.), *The Global/Local: Cultural Production and the Transnational Imaginary*. Durham, NC: Duke University Press.

Duff, Wilson. 1965. *Thoughts on the Nootka Canoe*. Victoria, BC: Queens Printer.

___. 1965b. *The Indian History of British Columbia (The Impact of the White Man)*. Victoria, BC: Province of British Columbia Department of Recreation and Conservation.

___. 1959. *Histories, Territories, and Laws of the Kitwancool*. Victoria, BC: British Columbia Provincial Museum.

___. 1952. "The Upper Stalo Indians of the Fraser Valley, British Columbia." *Anthropology in British Columbia: Memoir 1*. Victoria, BC: British Columbia Provincial Museum.

Elliot, W.C. 1931. "Lake Lillooet Tales." *Journal of American Folk-Lore* 44.

Elsey, C. 2009. "Embodied Versus Disembodied Identities: Shifting Markers Within the Canadian Aboriginal Experience." Paper presented at the Annual General Meeting of the Canadian Anthropological Society. University of British Columbia.

___. 2001. "Self, Body and World: A Phenomenological Re-Interpretation of British Columbia Ethnography of Aboriginal People." PhD thesis, Department of Sociology and Anthropology, Simon Fraser University.

___. 1997. "Report on Cultural Resources in Stein Valley Nlaka'pamux Heritage Park Background Document. Appendix 1." Kamloops, BC: Ministry of Environment, Lands and Parks.

Entriken, N. 1991. *The Betweenness of Place: Towards a Geography of Modernity*. Baltimore, MD: Johns Hopkins Press.

Evernden, N. 1985. *The Natural Alien: Humankind and Environment*. Toronto, ON: University of Toronto Press.

Feit, H. 1995. *Hunting and the Quest for Power: The James Bay Cree and Whitemen in the Twentieth Century, in Native Peoples: The Canadian Experience*. Second ed., edited by R.B. Morrison and C.R. Wilson. Toronto, ON: McClelland and Stewart.

___. 1986. "Hunting and the Quest for Power: The James Bay Cree and Whitemen in the Twentieth Century." In R.B. Morrison and C.R. Wilson (eds.), *Native Peoples: The Canadian Experience*. Toronto, ON: McClelland and Stewart.

Feld, S. 1996a. "A Poetics of Place: Ecological and Aesthetic Co-evolution in a Papua New Guinea Rain Forest Community." In Roy Ellen and Katsuyoshi Fukui (eds.), *Redefining Nature: Ecology, Culture, and Domestication*. London, ON: Routledge & Kegan Paul.

___. 1996b. "Waterfalls of Song: An Acoustemology of Place Resounding." In Steven Feld and Keith Basso (eds.), *Bosavai, New Guinea, in Senses of Place*. Sante Fe, NM: School of American Research Press.

___. 1982. *Sound and Sentiment: Birds Weeping Poetics and Song in Kaluli Expression*. Philadelphia, PA: University of Pennsylvania Press.

Fergussen, F. 1961. *Introduction, Aristotle's Poetics*. New York, NY: Hill and Wang.

Frideres, J., and R. Gadacz. 2005. *Aboriginal Peoples in Canada*. Toronto, ON: Pearson.

Friends of the Namiah Valley. 2012. Retrieved June 28, 2012, from <www.fonv.ca/thecourtcase>.

Galloway, B. 1993. *A Grammar of Upriver Halq'eméylem*. Berkely, CA: University of California Press.

Gell, A. 1995. "The Language of the Forest: Landscape and Phonological Iconism in Umeda." In Eric Hirsch and Michael O'Hanlan (eds.), *The Anthropology of Landscape*. Oxford, UK: Clarendon Press.

___. 1975. "The Metamorphosis of the Cassowaries." *London School of Economics Monographs in Social Anthropology* 51. London, ON: Athlone Press.

Gill, I. 2009. *All That We Say Is Ours: Guujaaw and the Re-Awakening of the Haida*. Vancouver, BC: Douglas and McIntyre.

Gitxan Chief's Office. 2010. Issue Papers. July 7. <www.gitxsan.com>.

Goldman, I. 1975. *The Mouth of Heaven: An Introduction to Kwakiutl Religious Thought*. New York, NY: Wiley.

Goldstein, K., and M. Scheerer. 1971. "Abstract and Concrete Behavior." In A. Gurwitsch (ed.), *Kurt Goldstein: Collected Papers*. The Hague: Martinus Nijhoff.

Greider, T., and L. Garkovich. 1994. "Landscapes: A Social Construction of Nature and the Environment." *Rural Sociology* 59, 1.

Groz, E. 1994. *Volatile Bodies*. Bloomington and Indianapolis, IN: Indiana University Press.

Hall, S. 1997. *The Local and the Global: Globalization*. Minneapolis, MN: University of Minneapolis Press.

Halpin, M. 1981. "'Seeing' in Stone: Tsimshian Masking and the Twin Stone Masks." In D. Abbott (ed.), *The World Is as Sharp as a Knife: An Anthology in Honour of Wilson Duff*. Victoria, BC: British Columbia Provincial Museum.

___. 1973. "The Tsimshian Crest System: A Study Based on Museum Specimens and the Marius Barbeau and William Beynon Field Notes." PhD Dissertation, University of British Columbia.

Hanna, D., and M. Henry. 1996. *Our Tellings: Interior Salish Stories of the Nlha7kapmx People*. Vancouver, BC: University of British Columbia Press.

Harris, K. 1999. "Implementing Dalgammukw: Biography of Ken Harris." *Institute of Indigenous Government* March.

Harris, M. 1966. "The Cultural Ecology of India's Sacred Cattle." *Current Anthropology* 7.

Harting, H. 2004. "Reading Against Hybridity? Post-Colonial Pedagogy and the Global Present in Jeannette Armstrong's Whispering in the Shadows." In C. Sugars (ed.), *Home-work: Post-Colonialism, Pedagogy and Canadian Literature*. Toronto, ON: University of Toronto Press.

Hayden, B. (ed.). 1992. *A Complex Culture of the British Columbia Plateau: Traditional Stl'atl'imx Economy*. Vancouver, BC: UBC Press.

Heidegger, M. 1972. *On Time and Being*. New York, San Francisco, London: Harper Torchbooks.

___. 1971a. "Building Dwelling Thinking." In M. Heidegger *Basic Writings, edited by D. Krell*, New York, NY: Harper and Row.

___. 1971b. "The Question Concerning Technology." In Martin Heidegger *Basic Writings*, edited by D. Krell. New York, NY: Harper and Row.

___. 1971c. "The Origin of the Work of Art." In M. Heidegger *Basic Writings*, edited by D. Krell. New York, NY: Harper and Row.

___. 1962. *Being and Time*. San Francisco, CA: Harper.

Hill-Tout, C. 1978a. "Notes on the N'tlaka'pamuq of British Columbia, a Branch of the Great Salish Stock of North America, 1899." In R. Maud (ed.), *The Salish People: Vol. 1*. Vancouver, BC: Talon Books.

___. 1978b. *The Salish People (The Local Contribution of Charles Hill-Tout), Volume I: The Thompson and Okanagan*. Vancouver, BC: Talon Books.

___. 1978c. *The Salish People (The Local Contribution of Charles Hill-Tout), Volume II: The Squamish and the Lillooet*. Vancouver, BC: Talon Books.

___. 1909. *The Shuswap, The Jesup North Expedition, Vol 2, Part vii*. New York: AMS Press.

___. 1904. "Ethnological Report on the Stseelis and Skaulits Tribes of the Halq'eméylem Division of the Salish of British Columbia." *Journal of the Anthropological Institute of Great Britain and Ireland* 34.

Hoffman, R. 2011. "Even Jesus Got Eleven Out of Ten: The Legacy of Joe Couture's Work within the Discipline of Native Studies." *The Canadian Journal of Native Studies* 31, 2.

Honoré, F., R. McCormick and M. Carmen-Rodríguez. 2006. *Counselling in the Aboriginal Community*. Victoria, BC: Department of Social Work, University of Victoria. <http://education2.uvic.ca/Faculty/hfrance/4%20culture.htm>.

Hudson, Douglas R. 2009. "Place-Centred Aboriginal Identity and the Discourse of Traditional Land Use in the Courts in BC." Canadian Anthropological Socieity, Annual General Meeting at Concordia University, Montreal, session titled "Emerging Indigenous Identities and the Land Question in Canada."

___. 2004. "The Okanagan." In R. Bruce Morrison and C. Roderick Wilson (eds.), *Native Peoples: The Canadian Experience*. Oxford University Press.

___. 1996. "The Okanagan." In C.R. Wilson and R.B. Morrison (eds.), *Native Peoples and the Canadian Experience*. Don Mills, ON: Oxford University Press.

___. 1987. "Nisga'a Land and Society: An Anthropologist's Perspective." A paper presented at the 2nd Tsimshian Research Symposium. Hartley Bay, B.C.

Hudson, D., 2009. "Place-Centred Aboriginal Identity and the Discourse of Traditional Land Use in the Courts in BC: Douglas R. Hudson." Paper presented to the Annual General Meeting of the Canadian Anthropological Society. University of British Columbia (May).

Hudson, D., and Marianne Ignace. 2004. "The Plateau." In B. Morrison and C. Wilson, eds, *Native Peoples: The Canadian Experience*. Third Rev. Edition. London: Oxford University Press.

Hudson, D., and Maurice DePaoli. 2000. "Excavation and the Six-Mile Site (DKRN5)." *The Midden* 32, 1.

———. 1999. "Archaeological Investigations at 6 Mile (DkRn 5), Lower Lillooet River." Report prepared for In-SHUCK-ch Services Society, Deroche, B.C. and Archaeology Branch, Province of BC.

Hurley, Mary C. 1999. "Aboriginal Treaty Rights." Parliamentry Research Branch, Law and Government Division, September 8. Revised July 13, 2000.

Idhe, D. 1976. *Listening and Voice: A Phenomenology of Sound*. Athens, OH: Ohio University Press.

Ignace, M. 1998. *Shuswap, in Handbook of North American Indians Vol. 12, Plateau*. Washington, DC: Smithsonian Institution.

Ingold, T. 1996. "Hunting and Gathering as Ways of Perceiving the Environment." In Roy Ellen and Katsuyoshi Fukui (eds.), *Redefining Nature: Ecology, Culture, and Domestication*. Toronto, ON: Berg Publishers.

Jenness, D. 1955. "The Faith of a Coast Salish Indian." *Memoir 3*. Victoria, BC: British Columbia Provincial Museum.

———. 1934–35. "The Saanich Indians of Vancouver Island." Manuscript No. VII-G-M8. Ottawa, ON: Canadian Ethnology Services National Museums of Canada.

Jensen, Derrick. 2004. Listening to the Land: Conversations about Nature, Culture and Eros. White River Junction, VT: Chelsea Green Publishing.

Jonas, H. 1966. *The Phenomenon of Life: Toward a Philosophical Biology*. New York, NY: Delta Books.

Kahn, M. 1996. "Your Place and Mine: Sharing Emotional Landscapes in Wamira, Papua New Guinea." In Steven Feld, *Senses of Place*. Seattle, WA: University of Washington Press.

Kennedy, D.I.D., and R. Bouchard. 2010. *The Lil'wat World of Charlie Mack*. Vancouver, BC: Talon Books.

———. 1992. "Stl'atl'imx (Fraser River Lillooet) Fishing." In Brian Hayden (ed.), *A Complex Culture of the British Columbia Plateau: Traditional Stl'atl'imx Economy*. Vancouver, BC: UBC Press.

———. 1978. "Fraser River Lillooet: An Ethnographic Summary." In Arnoud Stryd and Stephen Lawhead (eds.), *Reports of the Lillooet Archaeological Project, Archaeological Survey of Canada Paper No. 73*. Ottawa and Victoria: National Museums of Canada.

Kirk, R. 1986. *Wisdom of the Elders: Native Traditions on the Northwest Coast*. Vancouver, BC: Douglas & McIntyre.

LaForet, A. 1992. "Implementing Dalgammukw Conference Transcripts." *Biography of Ken Harris*. Burnaby, BC: Institute of Indigenous Government.

Landgrebe, L. 1984. "The Problem of Teleology and Corporeality in Phenomenology." In Bernhard Waldenfels, Jan Broekman, Ante Pazanin (eds.), *Phenomenology and Marxism*. [Routledge & Kegan Paul.] London, GB: Thetford Press.

———. 1977. "The Life-World and the Historicity of Human Existence." *Research in Phenomenology* XI.

Lepofsky, D. 1988. "Stein Valley Archaeology Assessment." Report prepared for the Nl'akapxm Nation Development Corporation.

———. 1986. "Archaeology Summary." *Stein River Heritage Summary and Evaluation*. Prepared for the Lytton and Mt. Currie Indian Bands.

Levi-Strauss, C. 1967. "The Story of Asdiwal." In Edmund Leach (ed.), *The Structural Study of Myth and Totemism*. Association of Social Anthropologists of the Commonwealth Monographs 5. London, GB: Tavistock.

Little Bear, L. 2002. *Naturalizing, Indigenous Knowledge: Synthesis Paper*. Saskatoon, SK: Aboriginal Education Centre, University of Saskatchewan.

M'Gonigle, M., and W. Wickwire. 1988. *Stein, the Way of the River*. Vancouver, BC: Talon Books.

Select Bibliography

Maaka, R., and C. Anderson. 2006. *The Indigenous Experience: Global Perspectives.* Toronto, ON: Canadian Scholars Press.

Macklem, P. 1993. "Ethnonationalism, Aboriginal Identities, and the Law." In M.D. Levin (ed.), *Ethnicity and Aboriginality: Case Studies in Ethnonationalism.* Toronto, ON: University of Toronto Press.

Maracle, L. 1990. *Oratory Coming to Theory.* North Vancouver, BC: Gallery Publications.

Maud, R. 1982. *A Guide to B.C. Indian Myth and Legend.* Vancouver, BC: Talon Books.

McHalsie, A.S. 2001. "Halqemelem Place Names in Stó:lō Territory." In K. Carlson (ed.), *A Stó:lō Historical Atlas.* Vancouver, BC: Douglas and McIntyre.

McMillan, A. 1988. *Native Peoples and Cultures of Canada.* Vancouver, BC: Douglas and McIntyre.

McMillan, A., and E. Yellowhorn. 2004. *First Peoples in Canada.* Vancouver, BC: Douglas and McIntyre.

Merleau-Ponty, M. 1968. *The Visible and the Invisible.* Evanston, IL: Northwestern University Press.

___. 1962. *Phenomenology of Perception.* New York, NY: Routledge and Kegan Paul.

Mills, A. 2005 [1994]. *Hang Onto These Words: Johnny David's Delgamuukw Evidence.* Toronto, ON: University of Toronto Press.

___. 1994. *Eagle Down Is Our Law: Witsuwit'en Law, Feasts, and Land Claims.* Vancouver, BC: UBC Press.

Mohs, G. 1993. "Sxwoxwiyam Stl'itl'aqem te Stó:lō Spirits of the Ancestors." Paper presented at the Society for American Archaeology Conference. St. Louis, MO.

___. 1990a. "Stó:lō Sacred Ground." Heritage Consultant's Report: Stó:lō Tribal Council.

___. 1990b. "The Upper Stó:lō Indians of British Columbia: An Ethno-Archaeological Review." Heritage Consultant's Report: The Alliance of Tribal Councils.

___. 1987. "Spiritual Sites, Ethnic Significance and Native Spirituality: The Heritage and Heritage Sites of the Stó:lō Indians of British Columbia." MA. thesis, University of British Columbia.

Munn, N. 1996. "Excluded Spaces: The Figure in the Australian Aboriginal Landscape." *Critical Inquiry* 22, 3 (Spring).

Musqueum website. 2006. "Musqueum: A Living Culture." <http://www.juliegordon.com/uploads/images/Musqueam_LivingCulture.pdf>.

Napoleon, V. 2005. "Delgamuukw: A Legal Straight Jacket For Oral Histories?" *Canadian Journal of Law and Society* 20, 2.

Neel, D. 1992. *Our Chiefs and Elders.* Vancouver, BC: UBC Press.

Nyman, E., and J. Leer. 1993. *Gagiwdulh: Brought Forth to Reconfirm. The Legacy of a Taku River Clan.* Whitehorse, YT: Yukon Native Language Centre, Fairbanks, AK: Alaska Native Language Center.

Parker, M.L. 1988. *Preliminary Dendrochronological Investigations in the Stein River Valley: Tree Age, Size, and Modification by Aboriginal Use.* Vancouver, BC: Western Canada Wilderness Committee.

Parker, P., and T. King. 1990. "Guidelines for Evaluating and Documenting Traditional Cultural Properties." In *National Register Bulletin 38.* Seattle, WA: National Park Service.

Peckerman, T.R., M. Fournier, M. Manheim and G. Listi. 2011. "Giving Voice to Canadian Aboriginal Peoples: A Collaboration Between Scholars and Aboriginal Communities." *Canadian Journal of Native Studies* 31, 1.

Rabinow, P., and W.M. Sullivan. 1979. *Interpretive Social Science.* San Francisco, CA: University of California Press.

Regan, P. 2010. *Unsettling the Settler Within: Indian Residential Schools, Truth Telling and Reconciliation in Canada.* Vancouver, BC: UBC Press.

Reimer, R. 2006. "Squamish Nation Cognitive Landscapes." Conference paper. Toronto, ON: Canadian Archaeological Association Publication.

____. 2003. "Squamish Nation Traditional Use of Nch'Kay on the Mount Garibaldi and Brohm Ridge Area." Draft reprint. Vancouver. <https://sites.google.com/site/pacificspiritart/articlespacificspiritart>.

____. 2000. "Extreme Archaeology: The Results of Investigations at High Elevation Regions in the Northwest." MA thesis, Dept of Archaeology, Simon Fraser University.

Ridington, R. 1988. *Trail to Heaven: Knowledge and Narrative in a Northern Native Community*. Iowa City, IA: University of Iowa Press.

Ross, R. 2006. *Dancing with a Ghost: Exploring Indian Reality*. Canada: Penguin Books.

Ruffo, A. 1999. "Why Native Literature?" In R. Hulan (ed.), *Native North America Critical and Cultural Perspectives*. Toronto, ON: ECW Press.

Schwager, Laura. 2003. "The Drum Keeps Beating: Recovering a Mohawk Identity." In Bonita Lawrence and Kim Anderson (eds.), *Strong Women Stories: Native Vision of Community Survival*. Toronto: Sumach Press.

Scott, C. 1989. "Knowledge Construction among Cree Hunters: Metaphors and Literal Understanding." *Journal de la Societe des Americanistes* LXXV.

Silko, L.M. 1996. *Yellow Woman and the Beauty of the Spirit: Essays on Native American Life Today*. New York, NY: Simon and Schuster.

Silver, Jim. 2008. "In Our Own Voices." Halifax, NS: Fernwood Publishing.

Smith, L.T. 1999. *Decolonizing Methodologies: Research and Indigenous Peoples*. Otago, NZ: University of Otago Press.

Sorflaten, L. 2006. "The Aboriginal Intellectual in Jeannette Armstrong's Whispering in Shadows: Between Indigenous Localism and Globalism." *Canadian Journal of Native Studies* 26, 2: 383–404. <http://www2.brandonu.ca/library/cjns/26.2/08Sorflaten.pdf>.

Squamish Nation. 2012. <www.squamish.net/aboutus/ourt.and.htm>.

Stein Valley Nlaka'pamux Heritage Park. 1997. "A Provincial Park-Management Plan Background Document." Ministry of Environment, Lands and Parks Division, Kamloops (March).

Sterrit, Neil J. 1998. *Tribal Boundaries of the Nass Watershed*. Vancouver: UBC Press.

Stoffle, R., D. Halmo, and D. Austin. 1995. *Cultural Landscapes and Traditional Cultural Properties: A Southern Paiute View of the Grand Canyon and Colorado River*. Tucson, AZ: Bureau of Applied Research in Anthropology, University of Arizona.

Strehlow, T.G.H. 1965. "Culture, Social Structure, and Environments in Aboriginal Central Australia." In Ronald Berndt (ed.), *Aboriginal Man in Australia: Essays in Honour of A.P. Elkin*. Sydney, AUS: Catherine Berndt.

Styrd, A., and M. Rosseau. 1996. "The Early Prehistory of the Mid Fraser-Thompson River Area." In Roy Carlson and Luke Bona (ed.), *Early Human Occupation in British Columbia*. Vancouver, BC: UBC Press.

Suzuki, David. 2006. *The Autobiography*. Vancouver, BC: Greystone Books.

Teit, J. 1972. *Tattooing and Face and Body Painting of the Thompson Indians*. Seattle, WA: Shorey Book Store.

____. 1930. "The Salishan Tribes of the Western Plateaus." *Annual Report of the Bureau of American Ethnology* 45.

____. 1917. "Tales from the Lower Fraser River, in Folk-Tales of Salishan and Sahaptin Tribes, edited by Franz Boas." *Memoirs of the American Folk-Lore Society* 11.

____. 1912a. "Notes on the Lillooet Indians of British Columbia." Lancaster, PA. (Copy at University of British Columbia, Special Collections.)

____. 1912b. "Mythology of the Thompson Indians." *Memoirs of the American Museum of Natural History* 12.

____. 1909. "The Shuswap." In *The Jesup North Expedition: Vol.2, Part VII*. New York, NY: AMS Press.

____. 1906. "The Lillooet Indians." In *Publications of the North Pacific Jesup Expedition: Vol. 2, Part V*. New York, NY: Leiden and New York.

____. 1900. "The Thompson Indians of British Columbia." *Memoirs of the American Museum of Natural History* 2, 4.

____. 1898. "Traditions of the Thompson Indians of British Columbia." *Memoirs of the American Folklore Society* 6.

____. 1896. "A Rock Painting of the Thompson Indians of British Columbia." *Memoir of the American Museum of Natural History* 8.

Teit, J., M.K. Gould, L. Farrand and K. Spinder. 1917. "Folktales of the Salishan and Sahaptin Tribes." *Memoirs of the American Folklore Society* 11.

Teit, J., H.K. Haeberlin and Lelen H. Roberts. 1928. "Coiled Basketry In British Columbia and the Surrounding Region." *Annual Report of the Bureau of American Ethnography* 41.

Tenant, P. 1990. *Aboriginal People and Politics: The Indian Land Question in British Columbia.* Vancouver, BC: UBC Press.

The Stein. 1988. Documentary Film. Vancouver, BC: Western Wilderness Committee.

Thom, B., and D. Bain. 2004. "Aboriginal Intangible Property in Canada: An Ethnographic Review." *Industry Canada.* <http://www.ic.gc.ca/erc/site/ippd-dppi.nst/eng/ipo/200.html>

Thornton, T. 1997. "Know Your Place: The Organization of Tlingit Geographic Knowledge." *Ethnology* 36, 4.

Tsleil-Waututh People of the Inlet. 2012. <http://www.burrardband.com>.

Turner, N., M. Boelscher-Ignace and R. Ignace. 2000. "Traditional Ecological Knowledge and Wisdom of the Peoples of British Columbia." *Ecological Applications* 10, 5.

Turner, N., M.T. Thompson, and A.Z. York. 1990. "Thompson Ethnobotany: Knowledge and Usage of Plants by the Thompson Indians of British Columbia." *Memoir 3.* Victoria, BC: British Columbia Provincial Museum.

Turpel, M.E. 1990. "Aboriginal People and the Canadian Charter: Interpretive Monopolies, Cultural Differences." *Canadian Human Rights Yearbook 1989–1990.* Ottawa: University Human Rights and Education Centre.

Warry, W. 2007. *Ending Denial: Understanding Aboriginal Issues.* Peterborough, ON: Broadview Press.

Weaver, Hilary. 2001. "Indigenous Identity: What Is It, and Who Really Has It?" *American Indian Quarterly* 25, 2 (Spring): 240–55.

Wells, O. 1987. *The Chilliwacks and Their Neighbours.* Vancouver, BC: Talon Books.

____. 1965. *A Vocabulary of Native Words in the Halq'eméylem Language as used by the Native People of the Lower Fraser Valley.* Sardis, BC: O.N. Wells.

Wickwire, W. 1991. "On Evaluating Ethnographic Representations: The Case of the Okanagan of South Central British Columbia." *Canadian Journal of Native Education* 18, 2.

____. 1989. *Write It on Your Heart, The Epic World of an Okanagan Story Teller/Harry Robinson.* Penticton, BC: Theytus Books.

____. 1988. "The Stein, Its People Speak." Report prepared for the Nl'akapxm Nation Development Corporation, Part One (September).

____. 1986. "Ethnographic Summary." In *Stein Heritage: Summary and Evaluation.* Report prepared for the Lytton and Mt. Currie Bands. On file with the band offices.

Wickwire, W., and M. M'Gonigle. 1995–96. "'Reading' Rock Art." *BC Studies* 108 (Winter).

____. 1991. "The Queens People: Ethnography or Appropriation?" *Native Studies Review* 7, 2.

Wickwire, W., and J. Teit. 1979. "Anthropologist of the People." *Nicola Valley Historical Quarterly* 2, 2.

Wilson, I. 1988 [1985]. "Stein River Haulroad Heritage Resources Inventory and Impact Assessment." Report prepared for BC Forest Products Ltd. Boston Bar, BC.

York, A., R. Daly and C. Arnett. 1993. *They Write Their Dreams on the Rock Forever.* Vancouver, BC: Talon Books.

Zaner, R. 1981. *The Context of Self: A Phenomenological Inquiry Using Medicine as a Clue.* Athens, OH: Ohio University Press.

Index

Index

poiesis, 10, 11, 12, 19, 20, 50-59, 62, 63,
  67, 69-81, 93, 95, 97, 99-111, 113,
  115, 117, 119, 120, 123, 124, 126
potlatch legislation, 15
private property, 7, 10, 41, 43, 92

Qua'qlqal brothers, 88

rationalism/rationalistic, 3, 22, 34, 38,
  46, 125, 126
real dwelling, 51, 79, 119, 123, 124
red cedar bark, 105, 107, 116
reflexive legitimating statement, 50, 59,
  77, 79
representation, 11, 34, 41, 45, 50, 59,
  62, 67, 69, 70, 85, 89, 91, 98, 105,
  111, 113- 115, 119-124
residential school, 7, 8, 15, 21, 118

sacred landmarks, 58, 63, 69, 75, 77-70,
  95, 98, 100, 104, 106, 119
Seaton Lakes, 82
section 35, 5, 14, 15, 20, 25, 28, 30, 32,
  34, 36, 37, 118, 119
Secwepemc, 14, 76, 77, 78, 80, 81, 87,
  88, 94, 102, 120
self-determination, 5, 18, 35, 36, 41
self-government, 6, 16, 22, 26, 27
self-identification, 6, 13, 19, 40-43, 49,
  52, 53, 61, 62, 67-71, 77, 104, 107,
  119-121
self, body, world, 4, 19, 20, 46, 49, 50,
  51, 53, 55, 57, 58, 60, 62, 67, 70,
  77, 79, 100, 103, 106, 109, 115,
  119, 122, 123,
selfhood, 3, 10, 11, 42, 45, 49, 50, 51, 53,
  58, 60, 61, 70, 71, 117, 120, 121,
  123, 126
Shalalth, 37
Shuswap, 37, 80, 81, 87, 93, 94, 102
Shwager, Laura, 22
Similkameen, 78, 88
sovereignty, 5, 6, 23, 30, 32, 35, 41, 127
Sparrow, 12, 20, 28, 29, 43
spek'tl, 79, 82, 87, 92, 99, 104
Spences Bridge, 88, 96
Squamish, 18, 84
Stl'atl'imx', 62, 76, 78, 80-83, 85-87, 92,
  94, 96, 100, 103, 104, 107, 119,
  120
Stó:lō, 62, 63, 67, 68
storyscape, 7, 10, 14, 19, 20, 22, 23, 41,
  49, 50, 52, 58, 61, 62, 68, 70, 75-

77, 78, 79, 81, 83, 87, 89, 91, 93,
  95, 97, 99, 119, 124,
Stryen Creek, 109
subject/object opposition, 3, 4, 10, 24,
  46, 47, 60, 125
Sweetie Malloway, 63
Sweetie's camp, 63, 64, 79, 106, 119

Taku River Tlingit, 19, 68, 69
Taku River, 19, 62, 68, 69, 79
Teit, James, 14, 34, 37, 48, 52, 76, 77,
  80, 81, 85-97, 102, 103, 136, 137
Tetlenitsa, Chief, 100
thematic anchors, 70
thematizations, 50, 57, 58
Thlee-sa, 87, 88, 92
Thompson River, 51, 76, 88, 89, 92-94,
  98
Thompson, The, 51, 76, 80, 88, 89, 92-
  94, 97, 98
three-fold structure, 9, 47, 123, 124
Tlingit, 19, 59, 68, 69, 70, 120, 130, 136
Tofino, 72
transformer tales, 3, 80, 82, 95
transformers, 3, 19, 48, 59, 62-65, 76,
  78-95, 97-99, 102, 119
treaty 8, 5, 25, 37, 47
treaty process, 1, 12, 25, 36, 37, 47, 117
Triangle, Brittany, 1, 20
Tsatzook, 108
Tsilhqot'n, 1
Tsimshian, 69, 71, 72
Tsleil-Waututh, 18

utilitarian, 4, 7, 10, 14, 15, 18, 22, 34-
  3841, 42, 45-47, 53, 118, 126

Vanderpeet, 20
Wamirans, 57
Vickers, Judge, 2

Western scientific thinking, 3, 125
white man's maps, 31, 34, 36, 42, 44, 118
whitestream, 6, 7, 27, 46, 59, 61, 118
wilp, 39, 69, 71, 72
worldview, 3, 4, 6, 9, 13, 23, 24, 29, 33,
  42, 43, 46, 90, 123, 124, 126

Xeni Gwet'in, 1, 2, 20

Yanyedi, s 68, 69, 79, 117
York, Annie, 47, 113, 114, 115, 116